Anonymous

One Hundred Choice Hymns in Large Type

Anonymous

One Hundred Choice Hymns in Large Type

ISBN/EAN: 9783337075972

Printed in Europe, USA, Canada, Australia, Japan

Cover: Foto ©Thomas Meinert / pixelio.de

More available books at **www.hansebooks.com**

INDEX OF FIRST LINES.

		PAGE
'Abide in Me!'—Most loving counsel this,	C. H. I.	118
Abide with me! fast falls the eventide,	LYTE.	150
A debtor to Mercy alone,	TOPLADY.	98
A mind at 'perfect peace' with GOD,	C. P.	85
And dost thou seem forsaken,	C. H. I.	131
Awake, my soul, and with the sun,	BP. KEN.	205
Beneath the Cross of JESUS,		148
Be PATIENT—life is very brief,		209
Bride of My Love! Ere from the Cross uplifted,	I. L. BIRD.	65
Child of GOD! believe His promise,	C. H. I.	123
Christian, when thy way seems darkest,	C. FENN.	203
Cling to the CRUCIFIED!	H. BONAR.	110
Come, thou weary sinner,	E. H. H.	140
Departed, say we? is it,	W. B. R.	215
Dread not the cup of sorrow,	C. H. I.	62
Faith is a very simple thing,	E. B.	29
FATHER, I ask for heavenly light,	H. A. B.	107
FATHER, I bring this worthless child to Thee,		125
FATHER, I know that all my life,	A. L. W.	72
Forth into the darkness passing,	H. A. B.	178
From the far-off fields of earthly toil,	P.	86
Give thanks in everything!	H. A. B.	44
Glory to Thee, My GOD, this night,	BP. KEN.	206
'Going home,' and going quickly!	C. F.	221
Hark, my soul! it is the LORD,	COWPER.	90
Hast thou within a care so deep,		35

5

INDEX OF FIRST LINES.

		PAGE
He gave me back the bond,		176
Heir of glory, art thou weeping?	C. H. I.	39
'Himself hath done it all.'—O how those words,	C. F.	33
How oft we pray for holiness,	C. H. I.	115
How sweet the name of JESUS sounds,	NEWTON.	102
I am far frae my hame, and I'm weary oftenwhiles,		174
I am seeking a country—the Home of the blest,	C. H. I.	41
I gave My life for thee,		217
I have a treasure which I prize,		13
I have been at the altar and witness'd the Lamb,		19
I have been to a land, a Border Land,	L. N. R.	137
I heard the voice of JESUS say,	H. BONAR.	109
I know not what may befall me,	BRAINERD.	219
I lay my sins on JESUS,	H. BONAR.	103
I need Thee, precious JESUS, for I am full of sin,	WHITFIELD.	105
In evil long I took delight,	NEWTON.	201
'In no wise cast thee out'—the words are spoken,	E. H. H.	111
I once was a stranger to grace and to GOD,	M'CHEYNE.	113
Israel, in ancient days,	COWPER.	199
Is thy cruse of comfort wasting? Rise and share it with another,		27
I shine in the light of GOD,		9
I thank Thee for the trials, LORD,	C. H. I.	46
'It may be in the evening,'	B. M.	165
It was a time of sadness, and my heart,	L. P. W.	185
I've found the Pearl of greatest price,	MASON.	23
I was wandering and weary,		158
I will bless Thee—for seasons of gladness,	C. H. I.	160

6

INDEX OF FIRST LINES.

		PAGE
Jesus, my Lord, I've told to Thee,	C. H. I.	127
Jesus, my Lord, to Thee I cry,	E. H. H.	83
Just as I am—without one plea,	C. ELLIOTT.	55
Just as thou art—without one trace,	R. S. COOK.	54
Just as Thou wilt—Lord, be it done,	C. H. I.	56
Lead me, my Father—lead Thy child,	C. H. I.	68
Lead, Saviour, lead; amid the encircling gloom,	I. H. N.	22
Let nothing keep you back from Christ,	E. H. H.	58
Look unto Me, and be ye saved,	E. H. H.	152
'Midst changing scenes and changing friends,	C. H. I.	180
Musing of all my Father's love,	H.	70
My day is dippin' in the West, 'tis gloamin' wi' me noo,		170
My Father, can I learn so hard a task?	E. J. A.	129
My hope is built on nothing less,	REES.	164
My Saviour, Thou hast offer'd rest,	E. H. H.	91
My weary spirit is oppress'd,	E. H. H.	79
Nearer, my God, to Thee,	S. F. ADAMS.	76
Nothing between, Lord, nothing between,	E. H. H.	162
Nothing, either great or small,	J. P.	133
O Christ, what burdens bow'd Thy head!	A. R. C.	52
O eyes that are weary, and hearts that are sore,		60
O Holy Spirit! now descend on me,	C. F.	11
O Lord, in me Thy mighty power exert,		15
Oh! call it not death—it is life begun,	E. E. H.	207
Oh, how can you live without Jesus, my friend?	E. J. A.	36
Oh! weep not for the blessed dead,	C. H. I.	191
Oh! yes, in all Thy dealings, Father,	C. H. I.	93
One by one the sands are flowing,		81
One sweetly solemn thought,	CAREY.	78

INDEX OF FIRST LINES.

		PAGE
Pilgrims on the road to glory,	. . .	172
ROCK OF AGES, cleft for me, . .	TOPLADY.	97
SAVIOUR, whose crown'd humanity, .	I. L. BIRD.	146
Softly and gently these words were breathed,	F. E. W.	196
'Soul, arise! Night's shades descending,'	I. L. BIRD.	16
Speak gently, it is better far, . . .	.	48
Still in loving, still in loving, more than being loved, is joy, . .	E. W.	31
'The Master has come over Jordan,' . .	.	25
The way is dark, my FATHER! cloud on cloud,	.	211
There is a Fountain filled with blood,	COWPER.	89
There is a Name I love to hear, . .	F. W.	135
There is life in a Look at the Crucified One, ...	A. M. HULL.	121
Thousands, O LORD of hosts! to-day, .	.	189
Thy way—not *mine*, O LORD, .	H. BONAR.	21
'Tis LOVE which hath our way prepared, .	.	99
To walk with GOD, O fellowship divine!	C. H. I.	100
We a' hae a something, be't great or be't sma',	W.	177
Wearied and worn with earthly cares, I yielded to repose, . . .	.	142
We wept—'twas *Nature* wept—but Faith, .	.	154
'We would see JESUS'—all is gloom around us,	.	156
We *would see* JESUS—for the shadows lengthen, . . .	.	50
What book is that, whose page divine, .	.	182
What then? Why then another pilgrim song, ...	J. C.	95
What think you of CHRIST? is the test,	NEWTON.	194
What Thou hast done, my GOD, for me,	C. H. I.	74

CHOICE HYMNS.

A Voice from Heaven.

SHINE in the light of God,
    His likeness stamps my brow;
Thro' the shadows of death my feet
    have trod,
But I reign in glory now!
    (Rev. xxi. 23; 1 John iii. 2; 1 Cor. xv. 55; Rev. xxii. 5.)

No fainting heart is here,
    No keen and throbbing pain,
No wasted cheek, where the frequent tear
    Hath roll'd and left its stain.
    (Matt. xxvi. 38; Job xxxiii. 16; Rev. xxi. 4; Psalm xlii. 3.)

I have found the joys of Heaven,
    I am one of the sainted band:
To my head a crown of gold is given,
    And a harp is in my hand!
    (Isa. xxxv. 10; Heb. xii. 22; 1 Peter v. 4; Rev. xiv. 2.)

I have learn'd the song they sing
    Whom Jesus hath set free;
And the glorious hills of Heaven resound
    With my new-born melody!
    (Isa. xxxviii. 20; John viii. 36; Isa. lx. 18; Rev. xv. 3.)

A VOICE FROM HEAVEN.

No sin—no grief—no pain,
  Safe in my happy home!
My fears all fled—my doubts all slain,
  My hour of triumph come!
(Isa. xxv. 8; John xiv. 2; Acts vii. 55; Rom. viii. 37.)

Oh! friends of mortal years,
  The trusted and the true,
Ye are walking still in the vale of tears,
  But I wait to welcome you.
(Prov. xvii. 17; 1 John i. 7; Heb. x. 36; Luke xvi. 22.)

Do I forget?—Oh no!
  For memory's golden chain
Still binds my heart to yours below,
  Till we meet and touch again.
(Mal. iii. 16; 2 Peter i. 15; 1 John iv. 7; 1 Thess. iv. 13.)

Each link is strong and bright,
  And love's electric flame
Flows freely down like a river of light
  To the home from whence I came.
(John i. 51; Daniel ix. 21; Rev. xxii. 1; 1 John iv. 9.)

Do ye mourn when another star
  Shines out from the glittering sky?
Do ye weep when the raging voice of war
  And the storm of conflict die?
(1 Cor. xv. 41; Daniel xii. 3; Deut. xxxii. 1; Mark iv. 39.)

Then why should your tears run down?
  And your hearts be sorely riven?
For another gem in the SAVIOUR's crown,
  And another star in Heaven?
(Luke viii. 52; Prov. xiv. 10; Isa. lxii. 3; Luke xxiii. 43.)

A Prayer for the Holy Spirit.

'If ye then, being evil, know how to give good gifts unto your children; how much more shall your heavenly Father give the HOLY SPIRIT to them that ask Him?'

HOLY SPIRIT! now descend on me
    As showers of rain upon the thirsty
        ground;
Cause me to flourish as a spreading tree;
    May all Thy precious fruits in me be found.

Be Thou my 'TEACHER'—to my soul reveal
    The length, breadth, depth, and height of
        JESUS' love;
And on my soul Thy blest instructions seal,
    Raising my thoughts and heart to things
        above.

Be Thou my 'COMFORTER'—when I'm distressed,
    O gently soothe my sorrows, calm my grief,
Help me to find upon my SAVIOUR'S breast,
    In every hour of trial, sure relief.

Be Thou my 'GUIDE' into 'all truth' divine;
    Give me increasing knowledge of my GOD;
Show me the glories that in JESUS shine,
    And make my heart the place of His abode.

A PRAYER FOR THE HOLY SPIRIT.

Be Thou my 'INTERCESSOR'—teach me how
  To pray according to GOD's holy will;
Cause me with deep and strong desire to glow,
  And my whole soul with heavenly longings fill.

Be Thou my 'EARNEST' of eternal rest,
  And 'witness' with me I am GOD's own child,
With His unchanging love and favour blest,
  By JESUS' Blood be fully reconciled.

Be Thou my 'SANCTIFIER'—dwell within,
  And purify and cleanse my every thought,
Subdue the power of each besetting sin,
  And be my will to sweet submission brought.

Be Thou my 'QUICKENER'—in me revive
  Each drooping grace so prone to fade and die;
Help me on JESUS day by day to live,
  And loosen more and more each earthly tie.

Blest SPIRIT! I would yield myself to Thee,
  Do for me more than I can ask or think;
Let me Thy holy habitation be,
  And daily deeper from Thy fulness drink.

C. F.

A Quiet Mind.

'My peace I give unto you.'—JOHN xvi. 27.

I HAVE a treasure which I prize;
    Its like I cannot find;
  There's nothing like it on the earth;
    'Tis this—A QUIET MIND.

But 'tis not that I'm stupefied,
    Or senseless, dull, or blind;
'Tis GOD's own peace within my heart
    Which forms my QUIET MIND.

I found this treasure at the Cross:
    And there, to every kind
Of weary, heavy-laden souls,
    CHRIST gives a QUIET MIND.

My SAVIOUR's death and risen life,
    To give it were designed;
His love's the never-failing spring
    Of this, my QUIET MIND.

The love of GOD within my breast,
    My heart to Him doth bind;
This is the peace of Heaven on earth—
    This is my QUIET MIND.

A QUIET MIND.

I've many a cross to take up now,
    And many left behind;
But present troubles move me not,
    Nor shake my QUIET MIND.

And what may be to-morrow's cross
    I never seek to find;
My SAVIOUR says, 'Leave that to Me,
    And keep a QUIET MIND.'

And well I know the LORD hath said,
    To make my heart resign'd,
That mercy still shall follow those
    Who have this QUIET MIND.

I meet with pride of wit and wealth,
    And scorn, and looks unkind;
It matters not—I envy none,
    While I've a QUIET MIND.

I'm waiting now to see my LORD,
    Who's been to me so kind;
I want to thank Him face to face,
    For this, my QUIET MIND

A Prayer for Daily Use.

Lord, in me Thy mighty power exert,
Enlighten, comfort, sanctify my heart;
Sweeten my temper, and subdue my will,
Make me like Jesus—with thy Spirit fill.

I want to live on earth a life of faith,
I want to credit all the Bible saith;
I want to imitate my Saviour's life,
Avoiding lightness, gloom, and sinful strife.

I want to bring poor sinners to Thy throne,
I want to love and honour Christ alone;
I want to feel the Spirit's inward power,
And stand prepared for death's eventful hour.

I want a meek, a gentle, quiet frame,
A heart that glows with love to Jesu's name:
I want a living sacrifice to be
To Him who died a sacrifice for me.

I want to *do* whatever God requires;
I want my heart to burn with pure desires;
I want to *be* what Christ my Lord commands,
And leave myself, my all, in His blest hands.

O Lord, impress Thine image on my soul;
My will, my temper, and my tongue control;
Lead me through life to glorify Thy grace,
And after death, to SEE THEE FACE TO FACE!

Soul, Arise!

'THE night cometh, when no man can work.'—JOHN ix. 4.

'Soul, arise! Night's shades descending
    Even now obscure the day,
Fast Life's priceless hours are spending,
    Christian to thy work! away!
Soldier! pledged beneath My banner
    All My foes to meet in war,
Pause not, till the loud Hosanna
    Hails My coming from afar.

Dwell not on the memories thronging
    Of the Past, with all its pain:
Cherish not a weary longing
    For the rest which shall remain.
Mourn not with a dreary spirit
    For the faithful gone to rest;
They My promises inherit,
    They with Me in light are blest.

Hear the trumpet tongue of Duty,
    Stay not for to-morrow's Sun;
Ere thine eyes behold My beauty,
    Much remaineth to be done.

SOUL, ARISE!

In Life's stormy battle ever
    Bear My name aloft in fight;
Thee from Me no foes can sever;
    Scorn the Wrong and work the Right.

Life to some is dark and dreary,
    Shifting scenes of toil and woe:
'Tis thy task to teach the weary
    Of a rest which all may know.
Children of a common Father,
    Aid the trouble-smitten poor;
Bear their burdens, all the rather
    That in them *I* seek Thy door.

Guide the wanderer in his blindness,
    Bid the lost of pardon hear;
Let no words but those of kindness
    Fall upon thy brother's ear.
Lowly o'er the dying bending,
    Cheer him in the closing strife
With the hope, from Heaven descending,
    Of the new and better life.

As the mourner's tears are flowing
    O'er the soul-abandoned clay,
Point him to the LORD bestowing
    Peace, which none can take away.

SOUL, ARISE!

There are woes which wait *thy* healing,
    Wounds which *thou* alone canst bind:
Hidden griefs which need unsealing,
    Lost ones whom I bid *thee* find.

Keep thy lamp at midnight burning,
    Lay not thou thine armour down;
Thou shalt wear at My returning
    Priestly robe and kingly crown.
Heed not though the world upbraid thee,
    I endured its scoffs alone;
I am ever near to aid thee—
    I confess thee for Mine own.

Pilgrim! though the road be dreary,
    It shall end in radiant light;
Be not of the pathway weary,
    Thou shalt walk with Me in white.
Soon will dawn a day immortal,
    Thou shalt share My victor throne,
And at Heaven's eternal portal
    For thy cross receive a crown.'

                              I. L. BIRD.

A Voice from the Altar of Burnt-offering.*

'THINE iniquity is taken away, and thy sin purged.'—
ISAIAH vi. 6-8.

 HAVE been at the altar and witness'd
    the LAMB
Burnt *wholly* to ashes for me;
And watch'd its sweet savour ascending on
    high,
    Accepted, O FATHER, by Thee.

And lo, while I gaz'd at the glorious sight,
    A voice from above reach'd mine ears:
' By this thine iniquity 's taken away,
    And no trace of it on thee appears.

' An end for thy sin has been made for thee
    here,
    By Him who its penalty bore:
With *blood* it is blotted eternally out,
    And I will not remember it more.'

---

* The burnt-offering, or Holah, means in Hebrew that which ascends.

A VOICE FROM THE ALTAR OF BURNT-OFFERING.

O Lord, I believe it, with wonder and joy—
  Confirm Thou this precious belief;
While daily I learn that I am, in myself,
  Of sinners the vilest and chief.

What Christ is, is now the unfolding to me
  Of the wonder of grace that I am;
And where He is seated, there also, I'm told,
  Is His loved one, the Bride of the Lamb.

Lord, send me on errands of mercy to those
  Who henceforth my path shall surround;
To tell them that sin, for which Jesus has died,
  May be sought for, but shall not be found:

That as far as the east is removed from the west,
  So far shall *their* guilt be removed,
Who have come to the altar, and learnt from Thee there,
  What the death of its Victim has proved.

Thy Way—Not Mine.

Thy way—not *mine*, O LORD,
　However dark it be!
　Lead me by Thine own hand;
Choose out the path for me.

Smooth let it be, or rough,
　It will be still the best;
Winding or straight, it matters not,
　It leads me to Thy rest.

I dare not choose my lot;
　I would not if I might:
Choose Thou for me, my GOD,
　So shall I walk aright.

The kingdom that I seek
　Is Thine; so let the way
That leads to it be Thine,
　Else surely I might stray.

Take Thou my cup, and it
　With joy or sorrow fill;
As best to Thee may seem,
　Choose Thou my good and ill.

Choose Thou for me my friends,
　My sickness or my health;
Choose Thou my cares for me,
　My poverty or wealth.

Not mine—not mine the choice,
　In things or great or small;
Be Thou my Guide, my Strength,
　My Wisdom, and my All.　H. BONAR.

Lead, Saviour, Lead.

'I will lead them in paths they have not known.'—
Isaiah xiii. 16.

Lead, Saviour, lead; amid the encircling gloom,
    Lead Thou me on.
The night is dark, and I am far from home;
    Lead Thou me on.
Keep Thou my feet; I do not ask to see
The distant scene—one step enough for me.

I was not ever thus, nor pray'd that Thou
    Shouldst lead me on:
I loved to choose and see my path: but now,
    Lead Thou me on.
I loved the glare of day, and, spite of fears,
Pride ruled my will:—Remember not past years!

So long Thy power hath bless'd me—sure it still
    Will lead me on,
O'er vale and hill, through stream and torrent, till
    The night is gone,
And with the morn, those angel-faces smile,
Which I have loved long since, and lost awhile.

I. H. N.

Christ Found.

I've found the Pearl of greatest price,
    My heart doth sing for joy;
And sing I must; a CHRIST I have—
    O what a CHRIST have I!

CHRIST is the Way, the Truth, the Life;
    The Way to GOD and Glory;
Life to the dead; the Truth of types—
    The Truth of ancient story.

CHRIST is a Prophet, Priest, and King;
    A Prophet full of light;
A Priest that stands 'twixt GOD and man;
    A King that rules with might.

CHRIST's manhood is a temple, where
    The altar GOD doth rest;
My CHRIST, He is the Sacrifice;
    My CHRIST, He is the Priest.

My CHRIST, He is the Lord of lords,
    He is the King of kings;
He is the Sun of Righteousness,
    With healing in His wings.

CHRIST FOUND.

My Christ, He is the Tree of Life,
  Which in God's garden grows;
Whose fruits do feed, whose leaves do heal;
  My Christ is Sharon's Rose.

Christ is my meat, Christ is my drink,
  My med'cine and my health;
My peace, my strength, my joy, my crown,
  My glory and my wealth.

Christ is my Father and my Friend,
  My Brother and my Love;
My Head, my Hope, my Counsellor,
  My Advocate above.

My Christ! He is the heaven of heaven!
  My Christ what shall I call?
My Christ is first, my Christ is last,
  My Christ is All in All!

MASON.

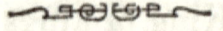

Christ and the Little Ones.

MARK x. 13; LUKE xviii. 15.

'The Master has come over Jordan,'
   Said Hannah, the mother, one day;
'He is healing the people who throng Him
   With a touch of His finger, they say.

'And now I shall carry the children,
   Little Rachel, and Samuel, and John;
I shall carry the baby Esther
   For the LORD to look upon.'

The father looked at her kindly,
   But he shook his head and smiled:
'Now who but a doting mother
   Would think of a thing so wild?

'If the children were tortured by demons,
   Or dying of fever, 'twere well;
Or had they the taint of the leper
   Like many in Israel.'

'Nay, do not hinder me, Nathan,
   I feel such a burden of care;
If I carry it to the Master,
   Perhaps I shall leave it there.

'If He lay His hand on the children,
   My heart will be lighter, I know;
For a blessing for ever and ever
   Will follow them as they go.'

CHRIST AND THE LITTLE ONES.

So over the hills of Judah,
    Along the vine-rows green,
With Esther asleep on her bosom,
    And Rachel her brothers between,—

'Mong the people who hang on His teaching,
    Or waiting His touch or His word,
Through the row of proud Pharisees listening,
    She pressed to the feet of her LORD.

' Now why shouldst thou hinder the Master,'
    Said Peter, ' with children like these?
Seest not how from morning to evening
    He teacheth, and healeth disease?'

Then CHRIST said, ' Forbid not the children!
    Permit them to come unto Me;'
And He took in His arms little Esther,
    And Rachel He set on His knee.

And the heavy heart of the mother
    Was lifted all earth-care above,
As He laid His hands on the brothers,
    And blest them with tenderest love:—

As He said of the babes in His bosom,
    ' Of such is the Kingdom of Heaven:'
And strength for all duty and trial
    That hour to her spirit was given.

'It is more Blessed to Give than to Receive.'

ACTS xx. 35.

Is thy cruse of comfort wasting? Rise and share it with another,
And through all the years of famine it shall serve thee and thy brother:
Love divine will fill thy storehouse, or thy handful still renew;
Scanty fare for one will often make a royal feast for two.

For the heart grows rich in giving; all its wealth is living grain;
Seeds (which mildew in the garner) scattered, fill with gold the plain.
Is thy burden hard and heavy? do thy steps drag wearily:
Help to bear thy brother's burden, GOD will bear both it and thee.

'IT IS MORE BLESSED TO GIVE THAN TO RECEIVE.'

Numb and weary on the mountain, wouldst thou sleep among the snow?
Chafe that frozen form beside thee, and together both shall glow.
Art thou stricken in life's battle? Many wounded round thee moan;
Lavish on their wounds thy balsams, and that balm shall heal thine own.

Is thy heart a well left empty? None but God its void can fill;
Nothing but a ceaseless fountain can its ceaseless longings still.
Is thy heart a living power? Self-entwined, its strength sinks low;
It can only live by loving, and by serving love will grow.

Faith in Jesus.

FAITH is a very simple thing,
    Though little understood;
It frees the soul from Death's
    dread sting,
By RESTING in the blood.

(1 Cor. ii. 14; Ex. xii. 13, 23.)

It looks not on the things around,
    Nor on the things WITHIN;
It takes its flight to scenes above,
    Beyond the sphere of sin.

(Jer. xvii. 9; Heb. i. 3.)

It sees upon the Throne of GOD
    A Victim that was slain;
It rests its ALL on His shed blood,
    And says, 'I'm born again.'

(Heb. x. 12, 14; 2 Cor. v. 15, 17.)

Faith is not what we FEEL or see,
    It is a simple TRUST
In what the GOD of Love has said
    Of JESUS as 'the Just!'

(1 John i. 9; 1 Pet. iii. 18.)

The PERFECT ONE that died for me,
    Upon His Father's throne,
Presents our names before our GOD,
    And pleads HIMSELF alone.

(Rev. iii. 21; Heb. iv. 14, 15)

FAITH IN JESUS.

What Jesus is, and that alone,
  Is faith's delightful plea;
It never deals with sinful self,
  Nor righteous self, in me.
    (Eph. i. 6, 7; Rom. vii. 18.)

It tells me I am counted 'dead'
  By God in His own Word;
It tells me I am 'born again'
  In Christ, my risen Lord.
    (Rom. vi. 6, 7; Rom. vi. 4, 5.)

In that He died, He died to sin;
  In that He lives—to God;
Then I am dead to Nature's hopes,
  And justified through blood.
    (Rom. vi. 10; Rom. iii. 24, 25.)

If He is free, then I am free
  From all unrighteousness;
If He is just, then I am just,
  He is my Righteousness.
    (Phil. iii. 20, 21; Eph. i. 17-23.)

What want I more to perfect bliss?
  A body like His own
Will perfect me for greater joys.
  Than angels round the throne.
    (1 John iii. 5-7; 1 Cor. i. 30, 31; 2 Cor. v. 21.)

F. B.

Love's Lesson.

TILL in loving, still in loving, more than being loved, is joy:
Here there lurks no disappointment, here is peace without alloy.

Not in having, or receiving, but in giving is there bliss;
He who has no other pleasure ever may rejoice in this.

Be it health, or be it leisure, be it skill we have to give;
Still in spending life for others Christians only really live.

What in love we yield to others, by a charm we still retain,
For the loved one's acquisition is the lover's double gain;

Yet we know in love's increasing is increase of grief and care,
For the pains of those around him, pained the loving heart must bear.

Love and sorrow dwelt together in the blessed Saviour's heart;
And shall we, His lowly followers, wish that they should be apart?

LOVE'S LESSON.

Love and sorrow walk together o'er this sin-beclouded earth :
Love and gladness sing together in the country of our birth.
Wheresoever sorrow wanders, love should go and raise her up ;
At the many wells of Marah love should stoop and share the cup.
Let the careless seek their pleasure, give, if e'er they give, their pelf;
But the loving, truly loving, gives, and loves to give, himself.
Happy if by his endeavour,—by his suffering others gain ;
If some comrade o'er his body may a wished-for height attain.
Secrets here of love and sorrow, if in meekness we shall learn ;
Secrets soon of love and gladness we in heaven shall discern.
In the light, so all-pervading, of the spirit's home above,
We shall trace the perfect meaning of the saying,—' GOD IS LOVE.'
And transformed to His likeness we, O blessed thought ! shall be
Loved and loving, loved and loving, through a bright eternity.
            E. W.

'Himself Hath Done It.'

ISAIAH xxxviii. 15.

'Himself hath done it all,'—O how those words
   Should hush to silence every murmuring thought!
Himself hath done it—He who loves me best,
   He who my soul with His own blood hath bought.

'Himself hath done it.'—Can it then be aught
   Than full of wisdom, full of tenderest love?
Not *one* unneeded sorrow will He send,
   To teach this wandering heart no more to rove.

'Himself hath done it.'—Yes, although severe
   May seem the stroke, and bitter be the cup,
'Tis His own hand that holds it, and I know
   He'll give me grace to drink it meekly up.

'Himself hath done it.'—O, no arm but His
   Could e'er sustain beneath earth's dreary lot;
But while I know He's doing all things well,
   My heart His loving kindness questions not.

'Himself hath done it.'—He who's searched me through,
   Sees how I cleave to earth's ensnaring ties;

'HIMSELF HATH DONE IT.'

And so He breaks each reed on which my soul
   Too much for happiness and joy relies.

'Himself hath done it.'—He would have me see
   What broken cisterns human friends *must* prove;
That I may turn and quench my burning thirst
   At His own fount of *ever-living* Love.

'Himself hath done it.'—Then I fain would say,
   'Thy will in all things evermore be done;
E'en though that will remove whom best I love,
   While JESUS lives I cannot be alone.'

'Himself hath done it,'—precious, precious words;
   'Himself,' my Father, Saviour, Brother, Friend;
Whose faithfulness no variation knows;
   Who, having loved me, loves me *to the end*.

And when, in His eternal presence blest,
   I at His feet my crown immortal cast,
I'll gladly own, with all His ransom'd saints,
'Himself hath done it,'—all, from first to last.

C. F.

Hast Thou a Care?

Hast thou within a care so deep,
It chases from thine eyelids sleep?
To thy REDEEMER take that care,
And change anxiety to prayer.

Hast thou a hope, with which thy heart
Would feel it almost death to part?
Entreat thy GOD that hope to crown,
Or give thee strength to lay it down.

Hast thou a friend, whose image dear
May prove an idol worshipped here?
Implore the LORD that nought may be
A shadow between Heaven and thee.

Whate'er the care which breaks thy rest,
Whate'er the wish that swells thy breast,
Spread before GOD that wish, that care,
And change anxiety to prayer.

How can You Live without Jesus?

H, how can you live without Jesus, my friend,
    That Saviour, so tender and true;
Whose love knows no measure, no change, and no end,
    And who offers it freely to you?

Is there never a season of sadness and pain,
    When your heart, in its desolate cry,
Complains that all human resources are vain,
    Its deeply felt need to supply?

Then how can you live without Jesus? One ray
    Of His Love would make sorrows depart
Like phantoms, before the bright dawn of the day
    That His smile would light up in your heart.

Is there never a time when, with pleasure's bright wine,
    Your glittering cup sparkles gay;

HOW CAN YOU LIVE WITHOUT JESUS?

And yet when your draught is the deepest you pine
  With a thirst it can never allay?

Then how can you live without JESUS? He gives
  Living water, of such healing power,
That he who drinks humbly for evermore lives,
  And never thirsts more from that hour!

Is there never a time, when your sins' heavy weight
  Seems to crush your soul down to despair,
And the threatening woes of Eternity's state
  With their terrors your spirit will scare?

Then how can you live without JESUS? Alone
  He can bear all your burden away.
No other escape! His blood must atone:
  His Life must your penalty pay.

Or, if you can live without JESUS, my friend,
  Will you venture without Him to *die?*
Alone, dare you enter the world without end?
  Stand alone in GOD's presence on high?

HOW CAN YOU LIVE WITHOUT JESUS?

And why should you live without Jesus? oh why!
    You have nothing to do but believe;
And why without Him should you venture to die,
    When He offers your soul to receive?

He is all that you need: He entreats you to come:
    Come at once—He invites you 'To-day,'
To-morrow may seal your Eternity's doom;
    At your peril you dare to delay.

No longer, then, live without Jesus, my friend!
    That Saviour so tender and true!
His love knows no measure, no change, and no end,
    And He offers it freely to you!

E. J. A.

Heir of Glory.

'IF children, then heirs; heirs of God, and joint-heirs with Christ.'—ROM. viii. 17.

HEIR of glory, art thou weeping?
  Why should tears bedim thine eyes?
Is there not a time of reaping
  Endless joys beyond the skies?

Are not all thy sins forgiven?
  Hast thou not the SPIRIT's seal?
Is not thine a home in Heaven?
  Dost not thou the earnest feel?

What, that's *passing*, heir of glory,
  Should thy blissful hopes obscure?
When the clouds of earth come o'er thee
  Look to JESUS! and endure.

See him there—for thee He's pleading;
  See thy name upon His breast:
He, the grace that thou art needing
  Will supply, and give thee rest.

Once for thee on earth He tarried,
  Worn, and weeping as He trod;
All thy sins and griefs He carried—
  His was love—the love of GOD!

Yes, that SAVIOUR, once so lowly,
  Now in Heaven for thee appears;
Sends His grace to make thee holy—
  Gives thee faith to calm thy fears.

HEIR OF GLORY.

Heir of glory, rise o'er sadness,
    What of earth is worth thy care?
Think upon the songs of gladness
    Thou shalt soon with angels share!

JESUS says, 'I'll never leave thee,'
    Heavenward He will safely guide;
Let not passing shadows grieve thee:
    Thou art safe when by His side.

Now with briers thy path is blended,
    For thy Heaven is not here;
Soon thy struggles shall be ended;
    GOD shall wipe away each tear.

Fix thine eyes on coming glory—
    Short the space that lies between;
For the joy that's set before thee,
    Slight the things that now are seen.

Soon thou'lt be with Him who bought thee,
    Live as one who knows His love;
Follow Him whose SPIRIT sought thee:
    Set thine heart on things above.

Soon thou'lt see His great salvation,
    Soon His smile shall shine on thee;
Though it be through tribulation,
    Sweeter then that rest will be.

In that region sweetest flowers,
    Fadeless, deathless, ever bloom;
There the joys that once were ours,
    Never wither in the tomb.   C. H. I.

I am Seeking a Country.

'AND confessed that they were strangers and pilgrims on the earth. For they that say such things declare plainly that they seek a country.'—HEB. xi. 13, 14.

AM seeking a country—the Home of the blest,
Where the wicked can't trouble, and the weary find rest;
Each day I am nearer that City of light,
And the thought is still dearer—the hope still more bright.

Like a pilgrim and stranger I onward would go,
Living loose to the world, and all its vain show;
And, if rough be my road, and thorny my way,
I will tread it the lighter, and with less delay.

Yes, when wild winds are howling, and dark is the sky,
I will hasten my steps to my Refuge on High;
For the storm and the tempest can there never come,—
Oh! there's nothing but sunshine in that happy Home.

If foes frown upon me—if friends should forsake—
If loved ones betray me—if riches wings take;

I AM SEEKING A COUNTRY.

Whatever my trial—whatever my woe—
I will try to forget it, and onward still go.

I am seeking a country, where all will be peace;
I am seeking a Home where earth's troubles shall cease;
There's no sorrow, no sickness, and no pain in Heaven,
And those who dwell there have their sins all forgiven.

Then joyfully, joyfully onward I'll go,
Forgetting the things that I once sought below;
As a pilgrim and stranger with glory in view,
I will take little heed of the way I pass through.

But I'll try that all those whom I meet on the road
May see I am seeking the 'City of God;'
I will try to make known all my SAVIOUR's great love,
Who now is preparing my mansion above.

I will tell them how ready He now is to save;
I will tell them how freely my sins He forgave;
I will try and compel them to come on with me,
That they of His glory partakers may be.

I AM SEEKING A COUNTRY.

Yes, I'll try that all those whom I meet on my way
May see I am living for that blessed Day,
When my LORD, and my King, in His glory shall come,
And take all His pilgrims to His happy Home.

As a heavenly stranger, with eyes fixed above—
With my heart still more full of my SAVIOUR's deep love;
May I walk through the world regardless of all
Those fleeting allurements which others enthral.

With Thee, O my GOD, for my Guardian and Guide,
Everywhere present—and close by my side;
Though lonely my path be, my heart shall not fear,
For nothing can harm me while Thou art near.

Then joyfully, joyfully upward I'll soar
Where I shall know sorrow and sin never more;
But where I my SAVIOUR shall love, serve, and see,
And with Him and His sainted ones ever shall be.

C. H. I.

'In Everything Give Thanks.'

GIVE thanks in everything!
    When life is summer bright,
    And all around thee seems to sing
An anthem of delight.
When thy cup runs o'er with bliss,
    Let thy lips run o'er with song,
Let thy heart, an offering free, be His
    Who hath fed thee all life-long.

Give thanks in everything!
    In the winter and the frost,
When thy buds of hope are withering,
    And thy dearest dreams are cross'd,
    Let Faith take up the strain,
        Praise from the wrung heart flow;
For the broken spells, and the kindly pain
    That forbids its rest below.

Give thanks in everything!
    Though thy portion be destroy'd,
Though the waters have fail'd from every spring
    And the store-house of bliss is void,
    The heart was slow to rise—
        Earth was too dear to thee—
'Twas a Hand of Love that loosed the ties;
    Sweeter thy rest will be!

Give thanks in everything!
    For 'all things' work thy good;
Thinkest thou thy LORD would *evil* bring
    On the soul He bought with blood?

'IN EVERYTHING GIVE THANKS.'

Thou wilt praise for all ere long,
    Retrac'd by the light of Heaven;
Hath Faith in the dark no trustful song,
    Ere open sight be giv'n?

  Give thanks in everything!
    For the cross He bids thee bear?
For the flow'rs beside thy path that spring,
    For the thorns that wound thee there;
  For the sunshine on the way,
    That makes thy journey sweet;
For the gloom descending while yet 'tis day,
    That urges on thy feet.

  Give thanks in everything!
    For the gifts He has denied;
For the gathering clouds that make thee cling
    More closely to His side.
  For the parting light of morn,
    For the length'ning shadows grey,—
Life's evening twilight is the dawn
    Of everlasting day!

  Give thanks in everything!
    For the call (whate'er it be)
That shall bid thy prison'd soul take wing
    Sav'd everlastingly!
  Faith, lost in vision bright!
  Shadows, in perfect day!
Fix *there* thy gaze, and the distant light
    Shall illumine all thy way.   H. A. B.

I Thank Thee, Lord.

'BLESSED is the man whom Thou chastenest, O Lord, and teachest him out of Thy law.'—Ps. xciv. 12.

'For He maketh sore, and bindeth up: He woundeth, and His hands make whole.'—JOB v. 18.

'Whom the Lord loveth He chasteneth.'—HEB. xii. 6.

'Blessed is the man that endureth temptation: for when he is tried, he shall receive the crown of life, which the Lord hath promised to them that love Him.'—JAMES i. 12.

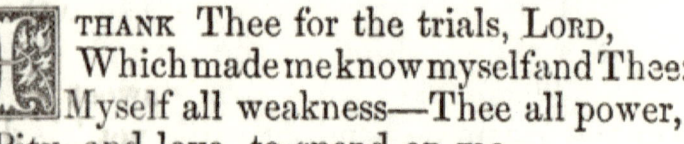

I THANK Thee for the trials, LORD,
  Which made me know myself and Thee:
  Myself all weakness—Thee all power,
  Pity, and love, to spend on me.

I thank Thee for each cord Thy love
  Hath cut, which kept me earthward bound;
And that in nothing but Thyself
  My happiness can now be found.

Closer, and closer, gracious LORD,
  To Thee, bind this poor weary heart!
Whate'er would come between, though dear
  Oh! spare it not, bid it depart.

Far off, above this passing scene,
  Oh! may my life with Thee be spent;
By earthly joys and woes unmoved,
  With Thine unchanging love content.

Sprinkled with Thy most precious blood,
  Thus saved, and set apart for Thee,
Anointed by Thy SPIRIT's power,
  Thus manifest Thy grace in me.

I THANK THEE, LORD.

This earth's poor husks my food no more,
  Higher and higher let me rise:
Till in the world I dwell like one
  Who looks upon it from the skies.
The past, the past, let it suffice
  To make me trust no other love;
But, LORD, I bless Thee for each wound
  That turned my wandering heart above;
And made me realise the truth
  That earth is not my resting-place;
Which rent the veil that came between,
  And hid from me Thy glorious face.
Thrice blessed chast'ning, that set free
  My spirit from its grovelling cell,
And taught it that alone in Thee
  True peace and endless pleasure dwell.
LORD, let me not find rest in aught
  But Thee—but Thee, my soul's true rest;
Forbid that I should ever lean
  On any but Thy loving breast.
Oh! by Thy SPIRIT's mighty power,
  So let me bask in light Divine,
That all transformed, from this hour,
  Thy likeness in my life may shine.
For it is joy, a joy like Heaven,
  To feel Thy SPIRIT on me rest;
To know my sins are all forgiven,
  And that my home is with the blest. c.h.i.

Speak Gently.

'LEARN of Me (saith Jesus); for I am meek and lowly in heart."—MATT. xi. 29.

PEAK GENTLY, it is better far
    To rule by love than fear;
  Speak gently, let not harsh words mar
    The good we might do here.
(1 John iv. 16; Neh. ix. 17; 1 John iv. 18; 1 John iii. 17.)

Speak gently, love should whisper low
    To friends when faults we find;
Gently let truthful accents flow;
    Affection's voice is kind.
(Isa. xlii. 2; Matt. xviii. 15; 1 Thess. ii. 7; Psalm cxli. 5.)

Speak gently to *the young*, for they
    Will have enough to bear;
Pass through this life as best they may,
    'Tis full of anxious care.
(Eph. vi. 4; 2 Tim. iv. 2; Gen. iii. 17; Job v. 7.)

Speak gently to *the aged one*,
    Grieve not the care-worn heart;
The sands of life are nearly run,
    Let such in peace depart.
(1 Tim. v. 1; Gen. xxxvii. 34; Lev. xix. 32; Gen. xliv. 31.)

SPEAK GENTLY.

Speak gently, kindly, to *the poor*,
    Let no harsh tones be heard;
They have enough they must endure,
    Without an unkind word.

<small>(Psalm xli. 14; Prov. xxxi. 26; 2 Chron. x. 7; Eph. iv. 31.)</small>

Speak gently to *the erring*, know
    That thou thyself art man;
Perchance unkindness made them so,
    O win them back again!

<small>(2 Tim. ii. 24; Eph. iv. 29; Luke vi. 35; Matt. xviii. 15.)</small>

Speak gently, for *'tis like the* LORD,
    Whose accents, meek and mild,
Bespoke Him as the SON OF GOD,
    The gracious Holy Child.

<small>(1 Peter ii. 21; Matt. xi. 20; John vi. 68; Luke iv. 22.)</small>

Wash'd in His Blood, redeemed to life,
    The family of Heaven
Flee from all anger, wrath and strife—
    Forgive, as they're forgiven.

<small>(1 Peter i. 18; 1 John v. 1; Titus iii. 2; Eph. iv. 32.)</small>

Hymn for the Evening of Life.

John xii. 21.

WE *would see* Jesus—for the shadows lengthen
 Across the little landscape of our life;
We would see Jesus, our weak faith to strengthen
For the last weariness, the final strife.

We would see Jesus—for life's hand hath rested,
 With its dark touch, upon both heart and brow;
And though our souls have many a billow breasted,
Others are rising in the distance now.

We would see Jesus—other lights are paling
Which for long years we have rejoiced to see;
The blessings of our pilgrimage are failing,
We will not mourn them—for we go to Thee.

HYMN FOR THE EVENING OF LIFE.

We would see JESUS—the great rock foundation
Whereon our feet were set by sovereign grace;
Not life, nor death, with all their agitation,
Can thence remove us if we see His face.

We would see JESUS—yet the spirit lingers
Round the dear objects it has loved so long,
And earth from earth can scarce unclose its
    fingers,
Our love to Thee makes not this love less
    strong.

We would see JESUS—sense is all too blinding,
And Heaven appears too dim—too far away.
We would see Thee—to gain a sweet reminding
That Thou hast promis'd our great debt to pay.

We would see JESUS—this is all we're needing,
Strength, joy, and willingness come with the
    sight;
We would see JESUS, dying, risen, pleading—
Then welcome day, and farewell mortal night.

The Suretyship of Jesus.

　Christ, what burdens bow'd Thy head!
　　Our load was laid on Thee;
Thou stoodest in the sinner's stead—
　Barest all my ill for me:
A Victim led, Thy blood was shed:
　Now there's no load for me.

Death and the curse were in our cup—
　O Christ, 'twas full for Thee!
But thou hast drain'd the last dark drop—
　'Tis empty now for me.
That bitter cup—love drank it up;
　Now blessings' draught for me.

The Father lifted up His rod—
　O Christ, it fell on Thee!
Thou wast sore stricken of Thy God;
　There's not one stroke for me.
Thy tears, Thy blood beneath it flow'd;
　Thy bruising healeth me.

The tempest's awful voice was heard—
　O Christ, it broke on Thee;
Thy open bosom was my ward:
　It braved the storm for me.
Thy form was scarr'd—Thy visage marr'd;
　Now cloudless peace for me.

THE SURETYSHIP OF JESUS.

A flame was kindled in God's ire—
  O Christ, it burned on Thee!
It was a hot, consuming fire,
  Ev'n in the fair green tree;
There did that fire feed and expire;
  Now it is quench'd for me.

Jehovah bade His sword awake—
  O Christ, it woke 'gainst Thee!
Thy blood the flaming blade must slake;
  Thy heart its sheath must be—
All for my sake, my peace to make:
  Now sleeps that sword for me.

The Holy One did hide His face—
  O Christ, 'twas hid from Thee!
Dumb darkness wrapt Thy soul a space—
  The darkness due to me.
But now that face of radiant grace
  Shines forth in light on me.

For me, Lord Jesus, Thou hast died,
  And I have died in Thee;
Thou'rt risen: my bands are all untied;
  And now Thou liv'st in me.
When purified, made white, and tried,
  Thy GLORY then for me!

A. R. C.

'The Saviour Bids Thee Come.'

UST as thou art—without one trace
Of love, or joy, or inward grace,
Or meetness for the heavenly place,
    O guilty sinner, come!

Thy sins I bore on Calvary's tree:
The stripes thy due were laid on Me,
That peace and pardon might be free—
    O wretched sinner, come!

Burden'd with guilt, wouldst thou be blest!
Trust not the world, it gives no rest;
I bring relief to hearts opprest—
    O weary sinner, come!

Come, leave thy burden at the Cross;
Count all thy gains but worthless dross;
My grace repays all earthly loss—
    O needy sinner, come!

Come hither! bring thy boding fears,
Thy aching heart, thy bursting tears;
'Tis mercy's voice salutes thine ears—
    O trembling sinner, come!

' The SPIRIT and the Bride say, Come,'
Rejoicing saints re-echo, Come;
Who faints, who thirsts, who will, may come:
    The SAVIOUR bids thee come!

R. S. C.

'O Lamb of God, I Come!'

Just as I am—without one plea
But that Thy Blood was shed for me,
And that Thou bidst me come to Thee,
    O Lamb of God, I come!

Just as I am—and waiting not
To rid my soul of one dark blot,
To Thee, whose Blood can cleanse each spot,
    O Lamb of God, I come!

Just as I am—though toss'd about
With many a conflict, many a doubt,
'Fightings within, and fears without,'
    O Lamb of God, I come!

Just as I am—poor, wretched, blind,
Sight, riches, healing of the mind,
Yea, all I need in Thee to find,
    O Lamb of God, I come!

Just as I am—Thou wilt receive,
Wilt welcome, pardon, cleanse, relieve;
Because Thy promise I believe,
    O Lamb of God, I come!

Just as I am—Thy love I own
Has broken every barrier down;
Now to be Thine, and Thine alone,
    O Lamb of God, I come!

Just as I am—of that free love
The breadth, length, depth and height to prove;
Here for a season, then above,
    O Lamb of God, I come!   C. E.

Just as Thou Wilt.

'Not my will, but Thine, be done.'—Luke xxii. 42.
'It is the Lord: let Him do what seemeth Him good.'—1 Sam. iii. 18.

Just as Thou wilt—Lord, be it done;
Perfect the work Thou hast begun;
Let all my heart and all my way,
Thy wisdom and Thy love display.

My portion Thou! and I am Thine!
Why should I ever then repine?
All must be right—all must be well—
For in Thy loving care I dwell.

Not my will, Lord, but Thine be done,
Till all my earthly course is run;
Since Thou hast given Thy life for me,
Be it my joy to live for Thee.

Each feeling of my heart and soul,
Do Thou, O Lord, alone control;
The cross Thou seest good for me,
Let me in meekness bear for Thee.

Oh! it will sweeten all my care,
To know that Thou hast placed it there;
To know Thy wisdom, love, and power,
Appoints my portion every hour.

JUST AS THOU WILT.

Thou wilt not send me any grief
But what *in Thee* can find relief:
The sorest wound that I can meet
Is heal'd when laid at Thy loved feet.

The struggle's o'er—I'm *willing* now
To all Thy discipline to bow:
At length Thy grace has made me see
My path is best as mark'd by Thee.

Enough to know that I am Thine;
And, precious SAVIOUR, Thou art mine:
Thou canst not err—Thou will not leave—
Nor willingly Thy servant grieve.

Then I will say that all is well,
And daily, LORD, Thy goodness tell:
Thy watchful eye can never sleep—
Thy strength, Thy weakest one will keep.

Just as Thou wilt—LORD, be it done;
Be Thou my Guard and Guide alone:
Let nothing, LORD, be given me,
But as it seemeth good to Thee.

C. H. I.

'Let Nothing Keep You Back.'

'LET nothing keep you back from CHRIST; I except nothing—neither sin nor sorrow.'

'The short way out of every difficulty is to carry it at once to JESUS, who is the opener of the seven seals.'

LET nothing keep you back from CHRIST,
   Nothing—without, within;
But spread at once before the throne
   Your sorrow and your sin.

And think not many words you need
   To make your meaning clear,
A *look* will carry all to Him,
   A *sigh* will reach His ear.

Even when a mist is cast around,
   And all seems dark to you,
It is as clear as light to Him
   With whom we have to do.

The 'far-off' thought He comprehends,
   He marks the silent tear,
And groans unutter'd bear to Him
   A message, deep and clear.

'LET NOTHING KEEP YOU BACK.'

He 'openeth the seven seals,'
    Solves each perplexing doubt;
And from our dark and crooked paths,
    He brings us safely out.

Regard not feeling, good or bad,
    Trust only what 'He saith;'
Looking away from all, to Him—
    This is to live by faith—

'Bare, naked faith,' that ventures all
    Upon the LORD alone,
Resting upon the *word* and *work*
    Of GOD'S ETERNAL SON.

And never shall our confidence
    To Him in vain be given;
Whate'er we *trust* Him with, on earth,
    We'll *praise* Him for, in Heaven.

E. H. H.

'Looking off unto Jesus.*'

EYES that are weary, and hearts that are sore,
Look off unto Jesus, and sorrow no more:
The light of His countenance shineth so bright,
That on earth, as in heaven, there need be no night.

'*Looking off unto Jesus,*' my eyes cannot see
The troubles and dangers that throng around me:
They cannot be blinded with sorrowful tears,
They cannot be shadowed with unbelief-fears.

'*Looking off unto Jesus,*' my spirit is blest,—
In the world I have turmoil—in Him I have rest:
The sea of my life all about me may roar,—
When I look unto JESUS, I hear it no more.

'*Looking off unto Jesus,*' I go not astray;
My eyes are on Him, and He shows me the way;

---

* This is the exact translation of Heb. xii. 2. 'Looking off [from all other objects] unto Jesus.'

'LOOKING OFF UNTO JESUS.'

The path may seem dark as He leads me along,
But following Jesus, I cannot go wrong.

'*Looking off unto Jesus,*' my heart cannot fear,—
Its trembling is still, when I see JESUS near;
I know that His power my safeguard will be,
For 'Why are you troubled?' He saith unto me.

'*Looking off unto Jesus,*' oh! may I be found,
When the waters of Jordan encompass me round :
Let them bear me away in His presence to be :
'Tis but seeing Him nearer whom always I see.

Then, then, I shall know the full beauty and grace
Of JESUS, my LORD, when I stand face to face :
I shall know how His love went before me each day,
And wonder that ever my eyes turned away!

The Father's Cup.

'THE cup which My Father hath given Me, shall I not drink it?'—JOHN xviii. 11.

'In the hand of the Lord there is a cup. . . . It is full of mixture.'—PSALM lxxv. 8.

DREAD not the cup of sorrow,
    Thy God that cup hath mix'd:
Think not of ills to-morrow,
    His love thy lot hath fix'd.

Thy FATHER? He arranges
    His children's portion here;
Through all life's weary changes,
    Be still, for He is near.

Then, trust the love of JESUS—
    So wise—so strong—so sweet—
He knows thy soul's diseases,
    The medicine that is meet.

Oh! hast thou been forsaken,
    Where most thy heart did cling?
That cup, thy Lord hath taken—
    He felt desertion's sting!

THE FATHER'S CUP.

Fear not though storms may lower,
   No wave can thee o'erwhelm;
While He, of mighty power,
   Directs, and holds the helm.

Each cloud—each stormy billow,
   But drives thee nearer home:
Thy harp take from the willow,
   And sing of joys to come.

Sing of the fadeless glory
   Which is prepared for thee:
Sing loud His love's sweet story
   Who all its light shall be.

Sing, for the days of sadness
   Are flying fast away:
Sing, for the home of gladness
   Is nearing day by day.

Sing, as each struggle's ended—
   The weary strife grows less!
Though tears with smiles are blended,
   Sing, and still onward press!

Sing, for when thou art weakest,
   He will His strength impart:
In grief, if Him thou seekest,
   He'll heal thy broken heart.

THE FATHER'S CUP.

If thou art sad and lonely,
   Sing, for thy LORD is near;
Trust Him, lean on Him, only,
   He'll wipe away each tear.

Sing, though thy heart is breaking,
   Praise will subdue its pain;
When a thorn its breast is aching,
   The bird* sings sweetest then.

As stars through night shine brightly,
   The past will seem to thee;
Then take earth's trials lightly,
   His love in all thou'lt see.

One hour of bliss in heaven
   Were worth long years of pain:
Happy to whom 'tis given,
   Through troubles, rest to gain.

Then though the path be dreary
   That leads thee to thy home,
Sing, when thy heart is weary,
   'LORD JESUS, quickly come!'

                           C. H. I.

---

* It is said that the nightingale sings sweetest when a thorn is piercing her breast.

Peace.

'PEACE I leave with you, My peace I give unto you; not as the world giveth, give I unto you.'—JOHN xiv. 27.

BRIDE OF MY LOVE! Ere from the Cross uplifted,
    The Heavens receive Me to My kingly throne,
MY PEACE I leave thee—not as earth bestoweth
    Her fading gifts, I give unto Mine own.

Child of My purchase! heir of fadeless glory,
    In tribulation great thou shalt be tried;
Yet in MY PEACE, which passeth understanding,
    Thy steadfast soul for ever shall abide.

MY PEACE I give thee—though to thy dim vision
    The narrow path in darkness fade away;
Strengthen thy falt'ring faith, the morn shall show thee
    My bleeding footprints on the rugged way.

PEACE shall be thine, though bitter mem'ries thronging,
    Of countless sins, across thy spirit roll;
Although the accuser of the holy brethren,
    With darkest doubts assail thy weary soul.

PEACE.

PEACE shall be thine, although 'life's fitful
    fever'
  Throb fiercely through thine aching head
    and breast,
And for thy soul's unrest and weary yearning,
  Earth has no balm or quiet ark of rest.

PEACE, when the feeble light by which thou
    steerest
  No longer glimmers from the further shore;
PEACE, when the loves and hopes long held
    the dearest,
  In the dark waves have sunk to rise no
    more.

PEACE, in the lonely hours of weary waiting,
  In valley twilight, cold, and sad, and
    grey;
Behold the mountain tops already rosy
  With the bright flush of the long looked-
    for day!

PEACE, in that loneliest, bitterest hour of
    anguish,
  Which bears thy loved ones from thy
    straining sight.
I am the endless Life, he that on Me believeth,
  In Paradise shall walk with Me in white.

PEACE.

Peace, in the day when death's cold waters swelling
　Around thy feet thy trembling soul affright;
The Hand that in the wilderness hath led thee
　Through the dark waves shall guide thee into light.

Peace, when the strange new sound of angel hymnings
　Breaks in wild music on thy wondering ear;
Peace, when thy human soul, unclothed and lonely,
　Before My throne in judgment shall appear.

Peace perfected, when, from the din of battle,
　The everlasting doors shall close thee in;
When thou shalt know, upon My throne beside Me,
　Victorious calm, freedom from strife and sin.

I. L. BIRD.

Lead Me, O Lord.

Psalm v. 8.

'I WILL lead them in paths they have not known: I will make darkness light before them, and crooked things straight. These things will I do unto them, and not forsake them.'—
ISAIAH xlii. 16.

LEAD me, my FATHER—lead Thy child,
   For I am blind, and cannot see
One step through this dark dreary wild;
   But I am safe while led by Thee.

Lead me, my FATHER—I am weak,
   And long and rugged is my way:
No strength have I—Thy strength I seek:
   While Thou art near no ills dismay.

Lead me, for I am foolish, FATHER,
   And know not what is best for me:
Nor what *I would*, but be it rather,
   Just as it seemeth good to Thee.

Lead me, for all is known to Thee,
   Each weary winding of my way;
What has been, and what yet shall be,
   The changes of life's changing day.

Wonderful! Counsellor! lead on;
   Nor let me faint, though trials deep
Should thicken, ere my race be run,
   Or I be called still more to weep.

LEAD ME, O LORD.

Lead on, and make me trust Thy love,
   Thy wisdom, tender care, and power;
Though Thou my faith shouldst deeply prove,
   Or dark temptations round me low'r.

Lead on, Thy wisdom cannot err—
   Unchanging is Thy precious love—
Unceasing is thy tender care—
   Thy power! what power can move?

Lead me, my FATHER, for I'm Thine—
   Thine own—Thy dearly purchased one;
Oh! through each cloud of darkness shine,
   Thy love to me in all make known.

Lead me, nor ever let me turn
   From paths of holiness aside;
Let grace within me brighter burn,
   Till all my sin is crucified.

Lead on, though hard the warfare be,
   Though friends be few, though foes be strong,
For I shall gain the victory
   (Which thou hast won for me) ere long.

Lead me, this is a foreign land!
   Oh! FATHER, leave me not alone;
Hold me by Thine all-powerful hand,
   Keep close to me, I am Thine own.

FATHER—SAVIOUR—GOD of power!
   Just as Thou wilt, still lead me on;
I would not choose, but hour by hour,
   Ask that Thy will in me be done.   C. H. I.

Meekly the Cup Receive.

'THE cup which My Father hath given Me, shall I not drink it?'—JOHN xviii. 11.

Musing of all my FATHER's love,
   (How sweet it is!)
Methought I heard a gentle voice:
  'Child, here's a cup—
I've mixed it—drink it up.'
My heart did sink—I could no more rejoice.

O FATHER, dost Thou love Thy child?
   Then why this cup?
'One day, My child, I said to thee—
  Here is a flower
Pluck'd from a beauteous bower:
Did you complain, or take it thankfully?

'One day I gave thee pleasant fruit
   From a choice tree:
How pleased, how grateful you did seem:
  You said—I love
Thee; faithful may I prove!
Your heart was full, with joy your eyes did beam.

MEEKLY THE CUP RECEIVE.

'That flower was Mine—that fruit was Mine—
    This cup is Mine,
And all that's in it comes from Me.'
    FATHER, I'm still;
Forgive my naughty will.
But what's the cup? may I look in and see?

'*You see*, My child! you must not see—
    CHRIST only saw
His destined cup of bitter gall:
    No, child, believe;
Meekly the cup receive,
And know that love and wisdom mix'd it all.'

    O FATHER, must it be?
      'Yes, child, it must.'
Then give the needy medicine,
    Be by my side,
Only Thy face don't hide:
I'll drink it all—it must be good—'tis Thine.

                    H.

My Times are in Thy Hand.

FATHER, I know that all my life
  Is portion'd out for me,
And the changes that are sure to
I do not fear to see: [come
But I ask Thee for a present mind,
  Intent on pleasing Thee.

I ask Thee for a thoughtful love,
  Through constant watching wise,
To meet the glad with joyful smiles,
  And wipe the weeping eyes;
And a heart at leisure from itself,
  To soothe and sympathise.

I would not have the restless will
  That hurries to and fro,
Seeking for some great thing to do,
  Or secret thing to know:
I would be treated as a child,
  And guided where I go.

Wherever in the world I am,
  In whatsoe'er estate,
I have a fellowship with hearts
  To keep and cultivate;
And a work of lowly love to do
  For the LORD on whom I wait.

MY TIMES ARE IN THY HAND.

So I ask Thee for the daily strength
   To none that ask denied,
And a mind to blend with outward life
   While keeping at Thy side;
Content to fill a little space,
   If thou be glorified.

And if some things I do not ask
   In my cup of blessing be,
I would have my spirit fill'd the more
   With grateful love to Thee—
More careful, not to serve Thee *much*,
   But to please Thee *perfectly*.

There are briers besetting every path,
   That call for patient care;
There is a cross in every lot,
   And an earnest need for prayer;
But a lowly heart, that leans on Thee,
   Is happy anywhere.

In a service which Thy will appoints
   There are no bonds for me;
For my inmost heart is taught the Truth
   That makes Thy children free;
And a life of self-renouncing love
   Is a life of liberty.   A. L. W.

No Love like Thine.

'COME and hear, all ye that fear GOD, and I will declare what
He hath done for my soul.'—PSALM lxvi. 16.

WHAT Thou hast done, my GOD,
    for me,
  Is more than I can tell;
This world had closed my heart to Thee,
  But THOU didst break the spell.

I cannot tell one-half Thy Love,
  Which, daily, LORD, I see:
Countless Thy tender mercies prove,
  Wondrous Thy Love to me.

But I would tell to all around
  That JESUS died for me;
That when in sin's dark bondage bound
  He set my spirit free.

Yes, I would tell how His pure Love
  Unchanging does remain;
And how He pleads for me above,
  In His most precious name.

NO LOVE LIKE THINE!

Would tell, how in my heaviest grief,
   He calms my soul to rest;
How He can give that heart relief
   Which leans upon His breast.

Would tell, how in life's loneliest hour,
   When every joy below
Seem'd wither'd like the fading flower,
   He sooth'd me in my woe.

Would tell, how in perplexing care
   He turns my thoughts above;
And makes me see that He is there
   Appointing all in Love.

Would tell, when weary oft with sin,
   And press'd beneath the load,
He by His SPIRIT's voice within,
   Points to my peace with GOD.

LORD, I would tell—how loudly tell!—
   There is no Love like Thine:
Thou ever wilt do all things well,
   THOU MIGHTY ONE, DIVINE.   C. H. I.

Nearer, My God, to Thee.

Nearer, my God, to Thee—
  Nearer to Thee,
E'en though it be a cross
  That raiseth me:
Still all my song shall be,
Nearer, my God, to Thee—
  Nearer to Thee.
(Psalm xlii. 1; Exod. xv. 2.)

Though like a wanderer,
  The sun gone down,
Darkness comes over me,
  My rest a stone;
Yet in my dreams I'd be
Nearer, my God, to Thee—
  Nearer to Thee.
(Gen. xxviii. 10-12.)

There let the way appear
  Steps unto Heaven;
All that Thou sendest me
  In mercy given.
Angels to beckon me
Nearer, my God, to Thee—
  Nearer to Thee.
(Gen. xxviii. 12, 13.)

NEARER, MY GOD, TO THEE.

Then with my waking thoughts,
   Bright with Thy praise,
Out of my stony griefs
   Bethels I'll raise;
So by my woes to be
Nearer, my GOD, to Thee—
   Nearer to Thee.
(Gen. xxviii. 18, 19.)

And when on joyful wing,
   Cleaving the sky,
Sun, moon, and stars, forgot,
   Upwards I fly;
Still all my song shall be,
Nearer, my GOD, to Thee—
   Nearer to Thee.
(Psalm xlii. 2; Psalm lxiii. 25.)

CHRIST alone beareth me
   Where Thou dost shine;
Joint-heir He maketh me
   Of the Divine!
In CHRIST my soul shall be
Nearest, my GOD, to Thee—
   Nearest to Thee.
(John xiv. 6; Rom. x. 19; Rom. viii. 17.)

S. F. ADAMS.

Nearer Home.

ONE sweetly solemn thought
    Comes to me o'er and o'er;
I'm nearer Home to-day
    Than ever I've been before.

Nearer my Father's House,
    Where the 'many mansions' be;
Nearer the great white throne,
    Nearer the jasper sea.

Nearer the bound of life,
    Where we lay our burdens down;
Nearer leaving the cross—
    Nearer gaining the crown.

But lying darkly between,
    Winding down through the night,
Is the dim and unknown stream
    To be cross'd ere we reach the light.

JESUS, perfect my trust,
    Strengthen the hand of my faith;
Let me feel Thee near when I stand
    On the edge of the shore of death;

Feel THEE near when my feet
    Are slipping over the brink;
For it may be I'm nearer Home—
    Nearer now than I think!   CAREY.

O Jesus, Set Me Free!

My weary spirit is oppress'd,
   It cannot rise to Thee;
Fetter'd by sin, and chain'd to earth,
   O JESUS, set me free!

From all the load of earthly cares
   That vex and harass me,
And from this weight of unbelief,
   O JESUS, set me free!

Round me I see a wide expanse
   Of light and liberty;
And yet my bonds I cannot burst,
   O JESUS, set me free!

LORD, open Thou my prison door,
   For Thou dost hold the key;
Utter the glad command, 'Go forth,'
   And then I shall be free.

Break Thou the chain of endless thought,
   It is too much for me;
Breathe rest throughout my weary frame,
   The REST OF TRUST IN THEE.

Reveal Thyself, LORD, to my heart,
   Thy glory let me see;
On JESUS fix my steadfast gaze,
   And then I shall be free.

O JESUS, SET ME FREE!

I'll hear what GOD the LORD will say,
   He will speak peace to me!
'Look unto *Me* and be ye saved,
   I set the prisoners free.

'No longer dwell within thyself,
   Look out from self to Me;
A full salvation I have wrought,
   And freely give to thee.

'Is there a good your heart can wish,
   That I've not bought for thee?
Take and enjoy what I have bought,
   And find your all in Me.

'Give up your thoughts, your thoughts are vain,
   They cannot profit thee;
They cannot change a single hair—
   Your wisdom is in Me.

'Bear not a single care yourself,
   One is too much for thee;
To work is Mine, and Mine alone—
   Your work is—REST IN ME.'

LORD, this is glorious rest indeed,
   To leave my all with Thee;
To cease from work, from care, from self—
   Oh, this is to be free!

                F.. H. H.

One by One.

'As thy days, so shall thy strength be.'—
DEUT. xxxiii. 25.

One by one the sands are flowing,
    One by one the moments fall;
Some are coming, some are going;
    Do not strive to grasp them all.

One by one thy duties wait thee;
    Let thy whole strength go to each;
Let no future dreams elate thee;
    Learn thou first what those can teach.

One by one (bright gifts from Heaven)
    Joys are sent thee here below;
Take them readily when given,
    Ready, too, to let them go.

One by one thy griefs shall meet thee;
    Do not fear an armed band;
One will fade as others greet thee,
    Shadows passing through the land.

ONE BY ONE.

Do not look at life's long sorrow,
  See how small each moment's pain;
God will help thee for to-morrow;
  Every day begin again.

Every hour that fleets so slowly
  Has its task to do or bear;
Luminous the crown, and holy,
  If thou set each gem with care.

Do not linger with regretting,
  Or for passion's hours despond;
Nor, the daily toil forgetting,
  Look too eagerly beyond.

Hours are golden links, God's token,
  Reaching Heaven; but, one by one,
Take them, lest the chain be broken
  Ere the pilgrimage be done.

'O Take Me as I Am!'

ESUS, my Lord, to Thee I cry,
　　Unless thou help me, I must die;
　　O bring Thy free salvation nigh,
　　　　And take me as I am!

Helpless I am, and full of guilt,
But yet for me Thy blood was spilt,
And Thou canst make me what Thou wilt,
　　　But take me as I am!

No preparation can I make,
My best resolves I only break,
Yet save me, for Thine own Name's sake,
　　　And take me as I am!

O Lord! Thine only would I be,
And yet I cannot go to Thee;
But, Saviour, Thou canst come to me,
　　　And take me as I am!

I thirst, I long, to know Thy love,
Thy full salvation I would prove;
But since to Thee I cannot move,
　　　O take me as I am!

Without Thee even prayer expires,
Fill then my soul with large desires,
And light it up with heavenly fires,
　　　But take me as I am!

'O TAKE ME AS I AM.'

Behold me, SAVIOUR, at Thy feet,
Deal with me as Thou seest meet;
Thy work begin, Thy work complete,
    But take me as I am!

SPIRIT of GOD, oh, breathe on me,
The SAVIOUR's glory make me see,
Changed to His image let me be,
    Come to me as I am!

Fall on me as the dews of even,
So silently, so freely given,
Show me *as free the things of Heaven*,
    Given to me as I am!

If Thou hast work for me to do,
Inspire my will, my heart renew,
And work both in and by me too,
    But take me as I am!

And when at last the work is done,
The battle o'er, the victory won,
Still, still my cry shall be alone,
    LORD, take me as I am!

E. H. H.

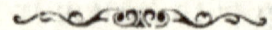

'Perfect Peace.'

A MIND at 'perfect peace' with GOD;
  Oh, what a word is this!
A sinner reconciled through Blood;—
  This, this, indeed, is peace!

By nature and by practice far—
  How very far!—from GOD;
Yet now by grace brought nigh to Him,
  Through faith in JESUS' Blood.

So nigh, so very nigh to God,
  I cannot nearer be;
For, in the Person of His SON,
  I am as near as He.

So dear, so very dear to GOD,
  More dear I cannot be;
The love wherewith He loves the SON—
  Such is His love to me.

Why should I ever careful be,
  Since such a GOD is mine?
He watches o'er me night and day,
  And tells me, 'Mine is thine.'

C. P.

The Harvest Home.

'THAT both he that soweth and he that reapeth may rejoice together.'—JOHN iv. 36.

From the far-off fields of earthly toil
    A goodly host they come,
And sounds of music are on the air—
    'Tis the song of the Harvest-Home.
The weariness and the weeping—
    The darkness has all pass'd by,
And a glorious sun has risen—
    The sun of Eternity!

We've seen those faces in days of yore,
    When the dust was on their brow,
And the scalding tear upon their cheek:
    Let us look at the labourers now!
We think of the life-long sorrow,
    And the wilderness days of care;
We try to trace the tear-drops,
    But no scars of grief are there.

There's a mystery of soul-chasten'd joy
    Lit up with sunlight hues,
Like morning flowers most beautiful,
    When wet with midnight dews.
There are depths of earnest meaning
    In each true and trustful gaze,
Telling of wondrous lessons
    Learnt in their pilgrim days.

THE HARVEST-HOME.

And a conscious confidence of bliss
    That shall never again remove,—
All the faith and hope of journeying years
    Gather'd up in that look of love.
The long waiting days are over;
    They've received their wages now;
For they've gazed upon their MASTER,
    And His name is on their brow.

They've seen the safely garner'd sheaves,
    And the song has been passing sweet,
Which welcomed the last in-coming one
    Laid down at their SAVIOUR's feet.
Oh! well does His heart remember,
    As those notes of praise sweep by,
The yearning, plaintive music,
    Of earth's sadder minstrelsy.

And well does *He* know each chequer'd tale,
    As He looks on the joyous band—
All the lights and shadows that cross'd their path
    In the distant pilgrim land;—
The heart's unspoken anguish,
    The bitter sighs and tears,
The long, long hours of watching,
    The changeful hopes and fears!

One hath climb'd the rugged mountain-side,—
    'Twas a bleak and wintry day;—
The tempest had scattered His precious seed,
    And He wept as He turned away.

THE HARVEST-HOME.

But a stranger-hand had water'd
   That seed on a distant shore,
And the labourers now are meeting,
   Who never had met before.

And *one*—he had toil'd amid burning sands,
   When the scorching sun was high:
He had grasped the plough with a fever'd hand,
   And then laid him down to die:
But another, and yet another,
   Had filled that deserted field,
Nor vainly the seed they scatter'd,
   Where a brother's care had till'd.

Some with eager step went boldly forth,
   Broadcasting o'er the land:
Some water'd the scarcely budding blade,
   With a tender, gentle hand.
There's *one*—her young life was blighted
   By the withering touch of woe;
Her days were sad and weary,
   And she never went forth to sow;

But there rose from her lonely couch of pain,
   The fervent, pleading prayer;
She looks on many a radiant brow,
   And she reads the answers there!
Yes! sowers and reapers are meeting;
   A rejoicing host they come!
Will you join the echoing chorus?—
   'Tis the song of the Harvest-Home! P.

Praise for the Fountain.

There is a Fountain filled with blood,
   Drawn from EMMANUEL's veins,
And sinners plunged beneath that
Lose all their guilty stains.   [flood

The dying thief rejoiced to see
   That Fountain in his day;
And there have I, as vile as he,
   Wash'd all my sins away.

Dear dying Lamb, Thy precious blood
   Shall never lose its power,
Till all the ransom'd Church of GOD
   Be saved, to sin no more.

E'er since, by faith, I saw the stream
   Thy flowing wounds supply,
Redeeming Love has been my theme,
   And shall be till I die.

Then in a nobler, sweeter song,
   I'll sing Thy power to save,
When this poor, lisping, stamm'ring tongue
   Lies silent in the grave.

LORD, I believe Thou hast prepared
   (Unworthy though I be)
For me a blood-bought, free reward,
   A golden harp for me!

'Tis strung, and tuned for endless years,
   And formed by power Divine,
To sound in GOD the FATHER's ears
   No other Name but Thine.   COWPER.

'Lovest Thou Me?'

Hark, my soul! it is the LORD;
   'Tis thy SAVIOUR, hear His word;
   JESUS speaks, and speaks to thee:
'Say, poor sinner, lov'st thou Me?

'I deliver'd thee when bound,
   And when bleeding, healed thy wound;
   Sought thee wandering, set thee right;
   Turn'd thy darkness into light.

'Can a woman's tender care
   Cease toward the child she bare?
   Yes, she may forgetful be,
   Yet will I remember thee.

'Mine is an unchanging love,
   Higher than the heights above,
   Deeper than the depths beneath,
   Free and faithful, strong as death.

'Thou shalt see My glory soon,
   When the work of grace is done;
   Partner of My throne shalt be:
   Say, poor sinner, lov'st thou Me?

LORD, it is my chief complaint,
   That my love is cold and faint;
   Yet I love Thee, and adore:
   O for grace to love Thee more!

COWPER.

'Rest.'

'IN returning and rest shall ye be saved; in quietness and in confidence shall be your strength.'—ISAIAH xxx. 15.

['I am lying like clay in the hands of the potter,' said an aged believer to his pastor. 'Ah! my friend, it is good to be there,' replied the pastor; 'when we lay ourselves thus in His hands, He alone knows how gloriously we shall come out of them.']

MY SAVIOUR, Thou hast offer'd rest,
  Oh! give it, then, to me;
The rest of ceasing from myself,
  To find my all in Thee.

This cruel self, oh, how it strives
  And works within my breast,
To come between Thee and my soul,
  And keep me back from rest.

How many subtle forms it takes
  Of seeming verity,
As if it were not *safe* to rest
  And venture all on Thee.

And yet it was no little price
  That bought this rest for me;
'Twas purchased at the mighty cost
  Of JESUS' agony.

'REST.'

I only enter on the rest
  Obtained by labours done;
I only claim the victory
  By Him so dearly won.

And LORD, I seek a *holy* rest,
  A victory over sin;
I seek that Thou alone shouldst reign
  O'er all, without, within.

In quietness, then, and confidence,
  SAVIOUR, my strength shall be;
And, '*Take me*, for I cannot *come*,'
  Is still my cry to Thee.

In Thy strong hand I lay me down;
  So shall the work be done;
For who can work so wondrously
  As an Almighty One.

Work on, then, LORD, till on my soul
  Eternal light shall break;
And in Thy likeness perfected,
  I, 'satisfied,' shall wake.

E. H. H.

Love Tokens!

'Whom the Lord loveth He chasteneth, and scourgeth every son whom He receiveth.'—Heb. xii. 6.

'If need be, ye are in heaviness through manifold temptations.'—1 Pet. i. 6.

Oh! yes, in all Thy dealings, Father,
    A 'need be' for each stroke I see;
From every chastisement I gather
    Fresh tokens of Thy love to me.

A foolish child, from Thee I wandered,
    And fondly clung to things of clay;
Earthly my heart and thoughts they rendered,
    And yet I could not break away.

With anguish oft my spirit smarted,
    Because I stray'd so far from Thee!
O smile upon me, now I've parted
    With all that once had charms for me.

Full many a chastening stroke I needed,
    To break the bonds that bound me here;
Thy mighty power at length succeeded
    To loose the spell once held so dear.

The bitterness of life is ended,
    For now my joy is found in Thee;
With Thee my every hope is blended,
    Thou'rt more than all the world to me.

No disappointment can o'ertake me,
    For Thy pure love no change can know;
Thou'lt never leave me, nor forsake me;
    With Thee I'm safe where'er I go.

LOVE TOKENS!

Lonely, yet not alone, my Saviour!
   While I can feel that Thou art near;
Life, light, and joy are in Thy favour:
   What can I want when thou art here?
What tho' the friends my fond heart cherished
   May now no longer on me smile;
Tho' hopes that once were bright have perished,
   With all that did my heart beguile;
They were but dreams, so vain, so fleeting,
   As mocks the heart that deems them true;
The tears at parting, smiles at meeting,
   Pass as the clouds or early dew.
While I can look on things unseen,
   Where dwells my Lord in changeless love,
I slight the griefs that intervene,
   And fix my gaze on things above.
Thou knowest, Lord, the earthward cleaving,
   That made my heart so dark, so dead;
Thou sawest the spell the world was weaving,
   That far from Thee I might be led.
In pity, Thou did give the fiat,—
   'Loosen her bonds; let her go free!'
Trembling—weeping—yet, Lord, by it,
   Risen from earth, I soar to Thee.
I bless the love that thus has broken
   The bonds I vainly tried to break:
I bless Thee, Lord, for every token
   That does my heart more heavenly make.

C. H. I.

'What Then?'

WHAT then? Why then another pilgrim song;
 And then a hush of rest divinely granted;
And then a thirsty stage, (Ah me, so long!)
 And then a brook, just where it is most wanted.

What then? The pitching of the evening tent;
 And then, perchance, a pillow rough and thorny;
And then some sweet and tender message, sent
 To cheer the faint one for to-morrow's journey.

What then? The wailing of the midnight wind;
 A feverish sleep; a heart oppressed and aching;
And then a little water-cruse to find
 Close by my pillow, ready for my waking.

'WHAT THEN?'

What then? I am not careful to inquire:
   I know there will be tears, and fears, and sorrow;
And then a loving SAVIOUR drawing nigher,
   And saying, '*I* will answer for the morrow.'

What then? For all my sins His pardoning grace;
   For all my wants and woes His loving-kindness;
For darkest shades the shining of GOD's face;
   And CHRIST's own hand to lead me in my blindness.

What then? A shadowy valley, lone and dim;
   And then a deep and darkly rolling river;
And then a flood of light—a seraph hymn—
   And GOD's own smile, for ever and for ever!

J. C.

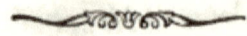

The Rock of Ages.

Rock of Ages, cleft for me,
Let me hide myself in Thee!
Let the water and the blood,
From Thy riven side which flowed,
Be of sin the double cure,
Cleanse me from its guilt and power.

Not the labour of my hands
Can fulfil Thy law's demands:
Could my zeal no respite know,
Could my tears for ever flow,
All for sin could not atone;
Thou must save, and Thou alone.

Nothing in my hand I bring,
Simply to Thy Cross I cling;
Naked, come to Thee for dress—
Helpless, look to Thee for Grace:
Foul, I to the Fountain fly;
Wash me, Saviour, or I die!

While I draw this fleeting breath,
When my eyelids close in death,
When I soar to worlds unknown,
See Thee on Thy judgment-throne—
Rock of Ages, cleft for me,
Let me hide myself in Thee!

TOPLADY.

The Assurance of Faith.

 DEBTOR to Mercy alone,
    Of Covenant-Mercy I sing;
Nor fear, with CHRIST's Righteousness on,
    My person and off'ring to bring.
The terrors of Law and of GOD,
    With me can have nothing to do;
My SAVIOUR's obedience and blood
    Hide all my transgressions from view.

The work which His goodness began,
    The arm of His strength will complete;
His promise is Yea and Amen,
    And never was forfeited yet.
Things future, or things that are now,
    Not all things below nor above,
Can make Him His purpose forego,
    Nor sever my soul from His love.

My name from the palms of His hands
    Eternity will not erase;
Impress'd on His heart it remains,
    In marks of indelible grace.
Yes! I to the end shall endure,
    As sure as the earnest is given;
More happy, but not more secure,
    The glorified spirits in heaven.

                    TOPLADY.

'Casting all your Care upon Him'.

1 Peter v. 7.

is Love which hath our way prepared,
And for our souls and bodies cared;
And Love sent each event.
No *chance* it is which trial sends,
'Tis Love which in our cup it blends,
And with most blest intent.
However bitter tastes the rind,
The kernel is of Love combined.

Ah! could we see that *faithful Hand*
Which such large store of good hath plann'd,
Of sorrow hath removed:
That Eye, which, seeing all so clear,
Hath guided us, now there, now here:
That Heart which hath so loved:—
Should we not be like children blest
Who in their mother's arms find rest?

A child is its own mother's joy;
To cherish it her sweet employ;
For it she seems to live.
Thus, Lord, is each of Thine Thy care,
As though Thine *only* child he were.
If this we would believe,
How sweetly trustful might we be,
Yea, Lord, in Thy blest care be free!

The Believer's Privilege.

'ENOCH walked with God.'—GEN. v. 24.

o walk with GOD, O fellowship divine!
  Man's highest state on earth—LORD,
    be it mine!
With Thee may I a close communion hold,
To Thee the deep recesses of my heart unfold:
Yes, tell Thee all; each weary care and grief
Into Thy bosom pour, till there I find relief.
O let me walk with Thee, thou Mighty One!
Lean on Thine arm, and trust Thy love alone;
With Thee hold converse sweet where'er I go;
Thy smile of love my highest bliss below!
With Thee transact life's business—doing all
With single aim for Thee—as Thou dost call:
My every comfort at Thy hand receive,
My every talent to Thy glory give;
Thy counsel seek in every trying hour,
In all my weakness trust Thy Mighty power.
Oh! may this high companionship be mine,
And all my life by its reflection shine.
My great—my wise—my never failing Friend,
Whose love no change can know, no turn, no
    end!
My SAVIOUR GOD! Who gavest Thy life for me,
Let nothing come between my heart and Thee!
From Thee no thought, no secret, would I keep,
But on Thy breast my tears of anguish weep.
My every wound to Thee I take to heal,
For Thou art touched with every pang I feel.

THE BELIEVER'S PRIVILEGE.

O, Friend of friends; the faithful, true and tried,
In Thee, and Thee alone, I now confide;
Earth's 'broken cisterns'—ah! they all have proved
Unsatisfying—vain—however loved;
The false will fail—the fondest, they must go!
Oh! thus it is with all we love below.
From things of earth then let my heart be free,
And find its happiness, my LORD, in Thee;
Thy HOLY SPIRIT for my Guide and Guest,
Whate'er my lot, I must be safe and blest;
Wash'd in Thy blood, from all my guilt made clean,
I in Thy Righteousness alone am seen;
Thy Home my home—Thy GOD and FATHER mine!
Dead to the world—my life is hid with Thine:
Its highest honours fade before my view—
Its pleasures, I can trample on them too.
With Thee by faith I walk in crowds—alone,
Making to Thee my wants and wishes known:
Drawing from Thee my daily strength in prayer,
Finding Thine arm sustains me everywhere;
While thro' the clouds of sin and woe the light
Of coming Glory shines more sweetly bright;
And this my daily boast—my aim—my end—
That my REDEEMER is my GOD—my FRIEND!

C. H. I.

The Name of Jesus.

How sweet the Name of JESUS sounds
    In a believer's ear!   [wounds,
It soothes his sorrows, heals his
    And drives away his fear.

It makes the wounded spirit whole,
    And calms the troubled breast;
'Tis manna to the hungry soul,
    And to the weary rest.

Dear Name! the rock on which I build,
    My shield and hiding-place;
My never-failing treasury, fill'd
    With boundless stores of grace.

JESUS! my Shepherd, Husband, Friend,
    My Prophet, Priest, and King;
My Lord, my Life, my Way, my End,
    Accept the praise I bring.

Weak is the effort of my heart,
    And cold my warmest thought;
But when I see Thee as Thou art,
    I'll praise Thee as I ought.

Till then, I would Thy love proclaim
    With every fleeting breath;
And may the music of Thy name
    Refresh my soul in death!

                              NEWTON.

The Fulness of Jesus.

'He was wounded for our transgressions, He was bruised for our iniquities.'—Isaiah liii. 5.

I LAY my sins on JESUS,
    The spotless LAMB OF GOD;
    He bears them all, and frees us
From the accursed load.
I bring my guilt to JESUS,
    To wash my crimson stains
White in His blood most precious,
    Till not a spot remains.

I lay my wants on JESUS,—
    All fulness dwells in Him;
He heals all my diseases,
    He doth my soul redeem.
I lay my griefs on JESUS,
    My burdens and my cares;
He from them all releases,—
    He all my sorrows shares.

THE FULNESS OF JESUS.

I rest my soul on JESUS,—
    This weary soul of mine ;
His right hand me embraces,
    I on His breast recline.
I love the name of JESUS,
    IMMANUEL, CHRIST THE LORD ;
Like fragrance on the breezes,
    His name abroad is pour'd.

I long to be like JESUS—
    Meek, loving, lowly, mild ;
I long to be like JESUS,
    The FATHER's Holy Child :
I long to be with JESUS,
    Amid the heavenly throng ;
To sing, with saints, His praises,
    To learn the angels' song.

H. BONAR.

The Heart of Jesus.

'UNTO you which believe HE is precious.'—1 PETER ii. 7.

I NEED Thee, precious JESUS, for I am full of sin,
My soul is dark and guilty, my heart is dead within:
I need the cleansing Fountain, where I can always flee—
The Blood of CHRIST most precious, the sinner's perfect plea.
(Zech. xiii. 1 ; 1 John i. 7 ; John i. 29 ; Eph. i. 7.)

I need Thee, precious JESUS, for I am very poor,
A stranger and a pilgrim, I have no earthly store :
I need the love of JESUS, to cheer me on my way,
To guide my doubting footstep, to be my strength and stay.
(Rev. iii. 18 ; Heb. xi. 13 ; Heb. xii. 1, 2 ; 1 Peter ii. 25.)

I need Thee, precious JESUS, I need a friend like Thee ;
A friend to soothe and sympathise—a friend to care for me :
I need the heart of JESUS, to feel each anxious care,
To tell my every want, and all my sorrows share.
(Heb. iv. 15, 16 ; Heb. xiii. 12.)

THE HEART OF JESUS.

I need Thee, precious JESUS, for I am very blind,
A weak and foolish wanderer, with a dark and
    evil mind :
I need the light of JESUS, to thread the thorny
    road,
To guide me safe to GLORY, where I shall see
    my God.
(2 Cor. xii. 9 ; John viii. 12.)

I need Thee, precious JESUS ; I need Thee day
    by day ;
To fill me with Thy fulness, to lead me on my
    way :
I need Thy HOLY SPIRIT, to teach me what I am,
To show me more of JESUS, to point me to the
    Lamb.
(Luke xi. 13 ; Col. ii. 9, 10.)

I need Thee, precious JESUS, and I hope to
    see Thee soon,
Encircled with the rainbow, and seated on
    Thy throne :
There, with Thy blood-bought children, my
    joy shall ever be,
To sing Thy praises, JESUS ; to gaze, my LORD,
    on Thee.
(Rev. iv. 3 ; Rev. vii. 9-17 ; Eph. iii. 20, 21.)

WHITFIELD.

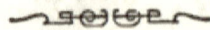

'Increase My Faith.'

FATHER, I ask for heavenly light
    To chase the mists of earth away:
    Time hides th' eternal from my sight:
  Increase my faith, I pray!

That, passing all that lies between,
    The cloud and sunshine by the way,
My eyes may rest on things unseen,
  Increase my faith, I pray!

That upwards, where my LORD has gone.
    My heart and hopes may rise each day,
Where He has led, my steps press on,—
  Increase my faith, I pray!

When threat'ning clouds are dense above,
    And storm and darkness hide Thy way,
That I may *trust*—nor doubt Thy love,—
  Increase my faith, I pray!

When, in the strain of wind and sea,
    The strands of hope well-nigh give way,
Haste, ere I sink, to succour me!
  Increase my faith, I pray!

When sins, o'erwhelming as a flood,
    Rise from the past in dread array,

'INCREASE MY FAITH.'

That I may trust th' all-cleansing blood,
   Increase my faith, I pray!

When lov'd ones pass within the vail,
   And leave me lonely on the way,
Lest heart, and hope, and courage fail,
   Increase my faith, I pray!

When, for the tears that dim my sight,
   I cannot trace their upward way,
Nor see them crown'd with saints in light,
   Increase my faith, I pray!

That through life's sorrow, care, and sin,
   And earth-born tumult, day by day,
Thy perfect peace may rule within,
   Increase my faith, I pray!

Mine be the eyes that through the night
   Wait patiently the dawn of day;
Mine be the trust that asks not sight—
   Increase my faith, I pray!

Till I have run my mortal race,
   Till the last shadows pass away,
Till glory crown Thy work of grace,
   Increase my faith, I pray!   H. A. B.

The Voice of Jesus.

'OF His fulness have all we received, and grace for grace.'—JOHN i. 16.

I heard the voice of JESUS say,
  Come unto Me and rest;
  Lay down, thou weary one, lay down
Thy head upon My breast.'*
I came to JESUS as I was,
  Weary, and worn, and sad;
I found in Him a resting-place,
  And He has made me glad.

I heard the voice of JESUS say,
  'Behold, I freely give
Thee living water—thirsty one,
  Stoop down, and drink, and live.'†
I came to JESUS, and I drank
  Of that life-giving stream:
My thirst was quench'd, my soul revived,
  And now I live in Him.

I heard the voice of JESUS say,
  'I am this dark world's Light;
Look unto Me, thy morn shall rise,
  And all thy day be bright.'‡
I look'd to JESUS, and I found
  In Him my Star, my Sun;
And in that Light of Life I'll walk,
  Till travelling days are done.   H. BONAR.

---
* Matt. xi. 28.   † John iv. 10.   ‡ John viii. 12.

Abide in Him.

Cling to the Crucified!
  His death is life to thee,—
  Life for eternity.
  His pains thy pardon seal;
  His stripes thy bruises heal;
  His cross proclaims thy peace,
  Bids every sorrow cease.
  His blood is all to thee,
    It purges thee from sin;
  It sets thy spirit free,
    It keeps thy conscience clean:
Cling to the Crucified!

Cling to the Crucified!
  His is a heart of love,
  Full as the hearts above;
  Its depths of sympathy
  Are all awake to thee;
  His countenance is light,
  Even in the darkest night.
  That love shall never change,
    That light shall ne'er grow dim;
  Change thou thy faithless heart,
    To find its all in Him:
Cling to the Crucified!

H. BONAR.

The Sure Refuge.

'HIM that cometh to Me I will in no wise cast out.'—JOHN vi. 37.

[An eminent divine, on his deathbed, said to a brother clergyman who was with him, 'In spite of all I have written, and all I have preached, there is but *one word* which gives me comfort now—it is this, "Him that cometh to Me I will in no wise cast out." Do you think I may venture my soul upon this promise?' 'If you had a thousand souls,' replied his friend, 'you might rest them all on this one word.']

'IN no wise cast thee out'—the words are spoken,
And, JESUS, never can Thy word be broken;
Here, then, I lay me down and take my rest,
Calm as an infant on its mother's breast.

'In no wise cast thee out'—O, words of power
To shed a light upon the darkest hour;
To meet each want I can on them rely,
And on their truth rest my eternity.

THE SURE REFUGE.

'In no wise cast thee out'—steadfast and sure
This anchor of the soul shall still endure;
Through life, through death, when heart and
    flesh shall fail,
Till it has brought me safe within the vail.

'In no wise cast thee out'—I need not care
To seek in this dark heart what is not there;
Alike from good or ill in self, I flee
To find my RIGHTEOUSNESS, my ALL, IN THEE.

'In no wise cast thee out'—I live, I die,
And, fearless, pass into eternity;
Resting on this alone, THY WORD IS GIVEN—
That word secures Pardon, Salvation, Heaven.

E. H. H.

Jehovah Tsidkenu.

'THE LORD OUR RIGHTEOUSNESS.'

ONCE was a stranger to grace and to God,
    I knew not my danger, and felt not
        my load;
Though friends spoke in rapture of Christ on
    the tree,
Jehovah Tsidkenu was nothing to me.

I oft read with pleasure to soothe or engage,
Isaiah's wild measure and John's simple
    page;
But e'en when they pictured the blood-
    sprinkled tree,
Jehovah Tsidkenu seem'd nothing to me.

Like tears from the daughters of Zion that
    roll,
I wept when the waters went over His soul;
Yet thought not that my sins had nailed to
    the tree
Jehovah Tsidkenu—'twas nothing to me.

When free grace awoke me, by light from on
    high,
Then legal fears shook me, I trembled to die;

JEHOVAH TSIDKENU.

No refuge, no safety in self could I see.—
JEHOVAH TSIDKENU my SAVIOUR must be.

My terrors all vanished before the sweet Name;
My guilty fears vanished, with boldness I came
To drink at the Fountain, life-giving and free:
JEHOVAH TSIDKENU is all things to me.

JEHOVAH TSIDKENU! my treasure and boast,
JEHOVAH TSIDKENU! I ne'er can be lost;
In Thee I shall conquer by flood and by field.
My cable, my anchor, my breast-plate and shield!

Even treading the valley, the shadow of death,
This 'watchword' shall rally my faltering breath;
For while from life's fever my GOD sets me free,
JEHOVAH TSIDKENU, my death-song shall be.

M'CHEYNE.

The Cup and the Crown.

'YE know not what ye ask. Are ye able to drink of the cup that I shall drink of?'—MATT. xx. 22.

'If so be that we suffer with Him, that we may be also glorified together. For I reckon that the sufferings of this present time are not worthy to be compared with the glory which shall be revealed in us.'—ROM. viii. 17, 18.

How oft we pray for holiness,
 Yet know not what we ask;
  We seek the heavenly prize to gain,
Nor think how hard the task!

Through sorrows deep the SAVIOUR trod,
 The sinner's life to gain:
His purchased ones must in His steps
 To heavenly joys attain.

Wouldst thou among the shining ones
 Be foremost in that place?
Or wear a brighter crown than all
 Who run the Christian race?

Then be assured thy path must be
 Through trials dark and deep;
Thine heart must oft be pierced with thorns,
 Thine eyes must ofttimes weep.

THE CUP AND THE CROWN

The soldier who would glory win
   Must bear the battle's strife —
Must wage through many a weary war,
   And yield but with his life;

Must free himself from every tie
   That had him homeward bound;
Must dash the tear drop from his eye,
   When fond ones cling around.

Wouldst thou above the things of earth
   On wings of rapture soar,
To hold communion in the heights
   Of bliss unknown before?

Then must the ties that bound thee here
   Be severed one by one;
And thy fond heart, loosed from them all,
   Contented, mount *alone*.

Oh! canst thou drink this bitter cup?
   He drank it once for thee!
He left His throne, and glorious ones,
   Thy Substitute to be!

Lonely to suffer, live, and die,
   To raise thee to His Throne;

THE CUP AND THE CROWN.

Then murmur not if thou, bereft,
　Shouldst tread to Heaven alone.

And think, whenever thou dost ask
　To be more holy here,
That if He grant to thee thy prayer,
　Some heart-sore trial's near.

The gem that decks the monarch's crown,
　Ere seen in beauty there,
Is hewn with many a cutting stroke,
　Its radiance to prepare.

Then count the cost: if thou wouldst shine
　A gem of heavenly ray,
The chisel deep must cut the dross
　That hides its light away.

But dark howe'er thy sorrows be,
　Or loud the storms that fall,
One glimpse of JESUS as He is
　Will make amends for all!

C. H. I.

Life in Jesus!

'ABIDE in Me, and I in you. As the branch cannot bear fruit of itself, except it abide in the vine; no more can ye, except ye abide in Me.'—JOHN xv. 4.

'He that saith he abideth in Him ought himself also so to walk, even as He walked.'—1 JOHN ii. 6.

'BIDE in Me!'—Most loving counsel this;
Nearest approach on earth to heavenly bliss.
With the command, O SAVIOUR, give me power
To live by faith in Thee, from hour to hour.

'Abide in Me!'—Sinner so poor and weak,
Vain is each other refuge thou wouldst seek;
Hidden in Me, thy sins are seen no more,
Blameless thou'lt stand the Judgment-seat before.

'Abide in Me!'—For I have strength to give,
The grace to make thee henceforth heavenward live;
Eternal things My Spirit can reveal,
And thy heart's earthly dark diseases heal.

LIFE IN JESUS!

'Abide in me!'—All else must change or die
Where thou dost fondest cling, or firm rely;
All else is shadow, which evades the grasp,
And mocks the heart whose tendrils round it clasp.

'Abide in me!'—All soon must pass away—
This earth so fair, these idols formed of clay;
Its riches, pleasures, friendships, pomp, and fame,
All evanescent are—all but a name!

'Abide in Me!'—For changeless is My love,
Its depths unmeasured, as its height above—
Not all thy feelings can its power repel:
Wilt thou not trust the love that loves so well?

'Abide in me!'—No ill can hurt thee there:
In Me thou'rt safe e'en from the Tempter's snare—
Before his fiery darts o'er thee prevail
My life must end, My faithfulness must fail!

'Abide in Me!'—If thou wouldst fruitful be:
The branch bears not when severed from the tree;
Without My Spirit's power, poor sapless bough!
No fruit thou'lt bear, for thou canst nothing do.

LIFE IN JESUS!

'Abide in Me!'—All grace is mine to give;
My voice the dead shall hear, and, hearing,
   live!
My Spirit can thy strongest sins subdue,
Soften thine heart, and all thy thoughts renew.

'Abide in Me!'—Live only on My love,
And thou shalt taste the bliss of saints above;
In Me thou shalt have peace; in Me find rest,
Though storms should rage around or cares
   molest.

'Abide in Me!'—Then safe within the vail,
Death cannot hurt, though heart and flesh
   may fail;
One with Myself, who vanquished death and
   hell,
It only breaks the bondage of thy cell!

'Abide in Me!'—Then thou mayst calmly
   smile
On ruined hopes, or ruined worlds the while;
Even the trumpet's awful sound shall be
The sweetest music ever heard, to thee.

C. H. I.

The Life-Look.

'He was wounded for our transgressions, He was bruised for our iniquities; the chastisement of our peace was upon Him; and with his stripes we are healed.'—ISAIAH liii. 5.

'Look unto Me, and be ye saved, all the ends of the earth.'—ISAIAH xlv. 22.

'Behold the Lamb of God, which taketh away the sin of the world.'—JOHN i. 29.

THERE is life in a LOOK at the Crucified One,
   There is life at this moment for thee;
Then look, sinner look, unto Him and be saved,
   Unto Him who was nailed to the Tree.

O why was He there as the bearer of sin,
   If on JESUS thy sins were not laid?
O why from His side flowed the sin-cleansing Blood,
   If His dying thy debt has not paid?

It is not thy tears of repentance, or prayers,
   But the Blood that atones for the soul:
On Him, then, who shed it, thou mayest at once
   Thy weight of iniquities roll.

THE LIFE-LOOK.

His anguish of soul on the Cross hast thou seen?
　　His cry of distress hast thou heard?
Then why, if the terrors of wrath He endured,
　　Should pardon to thee be deferred?

Thou art healed by His stripes,—wouldst thou
　　add to the word?—
And He is thy Righteousness made:
The best robe of Heaven He bids thee put on:
　　Oh! couldst thou be better arrayed?

Then doubt not thy welcome, since GOD has
　　declared
　　There remaineth no more to be done;
That once in the end of the world He appeared,
　　And completed the work He begun.

But take, with rejoicing, from JESUS at once
　　The Life Everlasting He gives;
And know, with assurance, thou never canst die,
　　Since JESUS, thy Righteousness, lives.

There is life in a LOOK at the Crucified One:
　　There is life at this moment for thee;
Then look, sinner look, unto Him and be saved,
　　And know thyself spotless as He.

M. A. HULL.

Thy Father's Love.

'We know that all things work together for good to them that love God, to them who are the called according to His purpose.'—Rom. viii. 28.

'If ye endure chastening, God dealeth with you as with sons.'—Heb. xii. 7.

Child of God! believe His promise,
   How dark soever be thy day;
That which seemeth most perplexing
   Shall thy Father's love display.

Child of God—through dangers passing,
   While no light gleams on thy path,
Trust the arm that still upholds thee;
   Care of thee thy Father hath!

Child of God—the furnace flaming,
   May for thee prepared be!
Tremble not, it cannot harm thee;
   A Father's love will watch o'er thee.

Child of God—though stormy billows
   Of dark temptation may abound;
Rest calmly, as on downy pillows,
   Thy Father's power will thee surround.

THY FATHER'S LOVE.

Child of God—bereft, forsaken,
  If such should be thy bitter lot!
Oh! let this thought thy joy awaken,
  Thy GOD, thy FATHER, changes not.

Child of God—has sickness laid thee
  On a weary bed of pain?
He who chastens, He has saved thee;
  Thy FATHER's grace will thee sustain.

Child of God—art thou left lonely?
  Are eyes that watch'd thee dimm'd and gone?
Are hearts now cold that loved thee warmly?
  Though lonely, thou art not alone.

Child of God—whate'er comes o'er thee,
  Think what thy portion soon shall be!
Think of the joy that's set before thee,
  When thou hast gained the victory!

Child of God—in joy and sadness,
  All must work for good to thee;
This thought should fill thy heart with gladness,
  My SAVIOUR died, and lives for me!

Child of God—soon, soon in glory
  Thou shalt His truth and wisdom see;
And with saints shall tell the story
  Of *all* the love He spent on thee. C. H. I.

The Intercessor.

John xvii.

ATHER, I bring this worthless child to
    Thee,
        To claim Thy pardon once; yet once
            again
Receive him at My hands—for he is Mine.
He is a worthless child; he owns his guilt.
Look not on him—he cannot bear Thy glance:
Look Thou on *Me;* his vileness I will hide.
He pleads not for himself—he dares not plead:
His cause is Mine—I am his Advocate.
By each pure drop of blood I lost for him,
By all the sorrows graven on My soul,
By every wound I bear, *I claim it due.*
Father Divine! *I cannot have him lost;*
He is a worthless soul, but *he is Mine.*
Sin hath destroyed him; sin hath died in Me:
Death hath pursued him; I have conquered
    Death:
Satan hath bound him; Satan is My slave.
My Father! hear him now—not him, but Me:
I would not have him *lost* for all the worlds
Thou for Thy glory hast ordained and made,
Because he is a poor and contrite child,
And all—his every hope—on Me reclines.
I know my children, and I know him Mine:

THE INTERCESSOR.

By all the tears he weeps upon My bosom,
By his full heart that beateth against Mine:
I know him by his sighings and his prayers,
By his deep trusting love which clings to Me.
I could not bear to see him cast away,
Weak as he is, the weakest of My flock—
The one that grieves Me most, that loves Me
    least:
I measure not My love by his returns;
And though the stripes I send to speed him
    home
Drive him, upon the instant, from my breast,
Still *he is Mine.* I drew him from the world.
He has no right, no home but in *My love.*
Though earth and hell against his soul conspire,
I shield him—keep him—*save him—we are one.*

O Sinner! what an Advocate hast thou!
Methinks I see Him lead the culprit in,
Poor, sorrowing, shamed, all tremulous with
    fear,
Prostrate behind his LORD, weak, self-condemned,
Clad with his SAVIOUR's spotless Righteousness,
Himself to hide, and hear the FATHER's words:
My Son! his cause is Thine, and Thine is Mine:
Take up Thy poor lost one—HE IS FORGIVEN.

'The Friend of Friends.'

'POUR out your heart before Him: God is a refuge for us.'—PSALM lxii. 8.
'And the Apostles gathered themselves together unto Jesus, and told Him all things.'—MARK vi. 30.

JESUS, my LORD, I've told to Thee
    Sorrows too deep for human ears;
But as I laid them at Thy feet,
    Thy love did stay my bitter tears.

Yes—LORD, and I have told to Thee
    Sins which I dare not others tell;
And while I poured them forth in prayer,
    Thy mercy did their guilt dispel.

My burdens, heavy to be borne,
    Thou, loving LORD, didst bear for me;
For Thou hast carried all my griefs;
    My sins' dark load was laid on Thee.

Oh! what a boon to have a Friend
    Who does each sin and sorrow know;
Almighty to subdue the sin,
    And pitying, to relieve the woe.

A Friend whom we may safely trust
    With every secret of the heart;
Who, when our wounds to Him we bring,
    Can His own healing balm impart.

Ah! in my weary days of woe,
    When wave of trouble roll'd o'er wave,

'THE FRIEND OF FRIENDS!'

What could sustain my sinking soul,
    But that He ready stood to save?

What? when the powers of darkness seemed
    Let loose to drive me to despair!
Where had I been? but that I then
    Could tell Thee all my griefs in prayer.

Where had I been? when all the earth
    To me was clothed in sable hue;
When 'friend and lover' Thou didst take,
    And hid them from my too fond view.

Where had I been? had not Thy grace
    Then turned my aching heart above!
And thence revealed Thyself to me,
    My living Friend—of changeless love!

Oh! Friend of friends! the truest, best,
    Whose love not all my sins can move;
Through varying scenes, unvarying Thou,
    My Rock, my Refuge, Thou dost prove.

No secret would I keep from Thee—
    No treasured sin from Thee conceal!
But the recesses of my soul
    To Thine all-pitying eyes reveal.

There's not a sin that grieves my heart,
    But Thou hast power to remove;
There's not a wound that I can feel,
    But has a balm in Thy deep love.   C. H. I.

'Though I be Nothing.'

2 Cor. xii. 11.

Y FATHER, can I learn so hard a task?
    You must; no more, my child, of
        you I ask,
Than He hath done—
My well-beloved SON.

Must I be nothing? Must I nothing do?
Nothing, my child: CHRIST hath done all
    for you.
You cannot buy,
The price is far too high,
Freely I give;—
Only 'Believe and Live.'

Enough—give Thou the humble heart, and
    I consent;
Oh, make me nothing, and therewith content.
My gain is loss,
My trust is in the Cross:
Hold me—I'm weak, I fall;
Be Thou mine—All in All.

'THOUGH I BE NOTHING.'

Here give me, LORD, some quiet place,
Where I can work, and yet behold Thy face:
While Thou wouldst have me stay,
Keep my feet steadfast in Thy way:
They must not tire
Till Thou shalt bid me 'Come up higher.'

I will be nothing still,
That CHRIST alone my heaven of heavens may fill.

Yet see me, LORD, a little glowing gem
Upon His diadem;
To shed my tiny ray
Among the splendours of His crowning day;
Though unperceived, I still should like to shine,
A tribute glory on that brow Divine.

And let me raise
One little note of praise,
Though scarcely heard among the myriad voices
When the redeemed Church above rejoices;
That it may blend
With angel Hallelujahs that ascend,
A lowly offering to my SAVIOUR—Friend.

LORD, I am nothing—CHRIST in all must shine;
Do with me as Thou wilt, for I am Thine.

E. J. A.

The Weary One Comforted.

AND dost thou seem forsaken,
    Poor weary one of woe?
Are all thy loved ones taken—
    Thy fairest hopes below?

Art thou a lone one waging
    The bitter war of life,
While sore temptations raging,
    More dreadful make the strife?

Oh! hapless, helpless, lone one,
    Just turn thine eyes above,
To One who won't abandon—
    To One of boundless love.

To Him who watches o'er thee,
    While passing through the fire;
Who bore it all before thee,
    And see thy heart's desire;

THE WEARY ONE COMFORTED.

To Him, the LORD of glory,
    Who knows thy feeble frame:
However sad thy story,
    Oh! trust thee in His Name.

The eternal GOD won't fail thee,
    However dark the storm;
Though fearful foes assail thee,
    Thy strength shall be His Arm.

Tell Him thy soul's deep sorrow,
    Tell Him thy griefs alone;
Whatever ills may harrow,
    Spread all before His throne.

He'll give thee strength, thou weak one,
    And take thee to His breast;
Will be thine all, thou lone one:
    He gives the weary rest.

And soon life's troubles ending,
    Will take thee to His home;
Then, on His love depending,
    'Fear not' whate'er may come.

C. H. I.

'What must I Do.'?

'SINCE I first discovered JESUS to be "the end of the law for righteousness to every one that believeth," I have more than once met with a poor sinner seeking peace at the foot of Sinai instead of Calvary (and coming as little speed as I did); and I have heard him now and again, in bitter disappointment and fear, groaning out, "What must I do?" I have said to him, "Do! do! what *can* you *do?* what do you *need* to *do?*"'

OTHING, either great or small,
    Nothing, sinner, no;
JESUS did it, did it *all*,
    Long, long ago.

When He, from His lofty throne,
    Stooped to *do* and *die*,
Everything was fully done;
    Hearken to His cry—

'It is finished!' Yes, indeed,
    Finished every jot;
Sinner, this is all you need;
    Tell me, 'Is it not?'

Weary, working, plodding one,
    Why toil you so?
Cease your 'doing,'—all was done
    Long, long ago.

Till to JESUS' work you cling
    By a simple faith,
'Doing' is a deadly thing,
    'Doing' ends in death.

WHAT MUST I DO?

Cast your deadly 'doing' down,
  Down at Jesus' feet;
Stand in Him, in Him alone,
  Gloriously complete!

The Resolution.

I'VE tried in vain a thousand ways
My fears to quell, my hopes to raise,
But what I need the Bible says,
     Is Jesus.

My soul is *night*, my heart is *steel*,
I cannot see, I cannot feel,
For light, for heat, I must appeal
     To Jesus.

He died, He lives, He reigns, He pleads,
There's love in all His words and deeds,
There's *all* a guilty sinner needs
     In Jesus.

Though some should sneer, and some
  should blame,
I'll go with all my guilt and shame,
I'll go to Him, because His name
     Is Jesus.

J. P.

The Name of Jesus.

There is a name I love to hear,
    I love to speak its worth;
    It sounds like music in mine ear,
The sweetest name on earth.

It tells me of a SAVIOUR's love
    Who died to set me free;
It tells me of His precious Blood,
    The sinner's perfect plea.

It tells me of a FATHER's smile
    Beaming upon His child;
It cheers me through this 'little while,'
    Through desert, waste, and wild.

It tells me what my FATHER hath
    In store for every day;
And though I tread a darksome path,
    Yields sunshine all the way.

It tells of One whose loving heart
    Can feel my deepest woe;
Who in my sorrow bears a part,
    That none can bear below.

THE NAME OF JESUS.

It bids my trembling soul rejoice;
    It dries each rising tear;
It tells me in a 'still small voice,'—
    To trust and never fear.

Jesus! the Name I love so well,
    The Name I love to hear!
No saint on earth its worth can tell,
    No heart conceive how dear.

This Name shall shed its fragrance still
    Along this thorny road;
Shall sweetly smooth the rugged hill
    That leads me up to God.

And there, with all the blood-bought
    throng,
    From sin and sorrow free,
I'll sing the new eternal song
    Of Jesus' love to me.
                              F. W.

The Border Land.

[THESE lines were sent by a lady to a friend who wrote frequently to know where she had been for several months, that she had not written to her. She had been to the gates of the grave, in a long and severe illness.] *Ellen Ranyard*.

I HAVE been to a land, a Border Land,
    Where there was but a strange, dim light!
Where shadows and dreams, in a spectral band,
    Seem'd real to the aching sight.
I scarce bethought me how there I came,
    Or if thence I should pass again;
Its morning and night were mark'd by the flight,
    Or coming, of woe and pain.

But I saw from this land, this Border Land,
    With its mountain ridges hoar,
That they look'd across to a wondrous strand—
    A bright and unearthly shore.
Then I turn'd me to Him, 'THE CRUCIFIED,'
    In most humble faith and prayer,
Who had ransom'd with Blood my sinful soul,
    For I thought He would call me there.

THE BORDER LAND.

Yet nay; for awhile in the Border Land
    He bade me in patience stay,
And gather rich fruits with a trembling hand,
    Whilst He chased its gloom away:
He had led me amid those shadows dim,
    And shown that bright world so near,
To teach me that earnest trust in Him
    Is 'the one thing needful' here.

And so from the land, the Border Land,
    I have turn'd me to earth once more!
But earth and its works were such trifles, scann'd
    By the light of that radiant shore.
And, oh! should they ever possess me again
    Too deeply in heart and hand,
I must think how empty they seem'd, and vain,
    From the heights of the Border Land.

The Border Land had depths and vales,
    Where sorrow for sin was known;
Where small seem'd great, as weigh'd in scales
    Held by GOD's hand alone.
'Twas a land where earthly pride was nought,
    Where the poor were brought to mind,
With the scanty bed, their fireless cot,
    And their bread so hard to find.

But little I heard in the Border Land
    Of all that pass'd below;
The once loud voices of human life
    To the deafen'd ear were low.

THE BORDER LAND.

I was deaf to the clang of its trumpet call,
    And alike to its gibe or its sneer;
Its riches were dust, and the loss of all
    Would then scarce have cost a tear.

I met with a Friend in this Border Land,
    Whose teachings can come with power
To the blinded eye and the deafen'd ear,
    In affliction's loneliest hour.
'Times of refreshing' to the soul,
    In languor, oft He brings,
Prepares it then to meditate
    On high and glorious things.

Oh! HOLY GHOST! too often grieved
    In health and earthly haste,
I bless those slow and silent hours
    Which seem'd to run to waste.
I would not *but* have pass'd those 'depths,'
    And such communion known,
As can be held in the Border Land
    With Thee, and Thee alone.

I have been to a land, a Border Land!
    May oblivion never roll
O'er the mighty lessons which there and then
    Have been graven on my soul!
I have trodden a path I did not know,
    Safe in my SAVIOUR's hand:
I can trust Him for all the future, now
    I have been to the Border Land.   L. N. R.

The Weary One Invited.

'COME unto Me, all ye that labour and are heavy laden, and I will give you rest.'—MATT. xi. 28.

COME, thou weary sinner,
    Look to ME and live,
    Free and full salvation
Now is MINE to give.

Is thy sin still twining
    Chains too strong for thee?
I can burst the strongest—
    Bring them all to ME.

Do anxious thoughts distress thee—
    Cares that know no balm?
I can hush each tempest
    Into perfect calm.

Lean thy head, thou tired one,
    Lean it on MY breast,—
There, whate'er thy burden,
    Thou shalt find a rest.

Lo, the Ark is open!
    Come, thou weary dove,
Rest from all thy wanderings
    In MY heart of love.

THE WEARY ONE INVITED.

Is thy plumage broken,
    Soiled by woe and sin?
See the FOUNTAIN opened—
    Plunge thou freely in!

White as snow untrodden
    Then thou shalt become;
'Wings of silver' bear thee
    Upward to thy Home.

There, in calm unbroken,
    Thou shalt rest with ME;
Hush'd to glassy stillness
    Life's tempestuous sea.

SAVIOUR, I am willing!
    At Thy feet I bow;
Body, soul, and spirit,
    Take, O take me *now!*

Let Thy love's full glory
    Shine upon my heart;
Bind me closely to Thee,
    Never to depart.

To Thy blessed service
    Let my life be given;
Then—Thy work completed,
    Take me to Thy heaven.   E. H. H.

The Starless Crown.

'THEY that turn many to righteousness shall shine as the stars for ever and ever.'—DANIEL xii. 3.

EARIED and worn with earthly cares,
   I yielded to repose,
   And soon before my raptured sight a glorious vision rose:
I thought, whilst slumbering on my couch, in midnight's solemn gloom,
I heard an angel's silvery voice, and radiance fill'd my room.
A gentle touch awakened me,—a gentle whisper said,
'Arise, O sleeper, follow me;' and through the air we fled.
We left the earth so far away, that like a speck it seem'd,
And heavenly glory, calm and pure, across our pathway stream'd.
Still on we went,—my soul was rapt in silent ecstasy;
I wonder'd what the end would be, what next should meet mine eye.

THE STARLESS CROWN.

I knew not how we journey'd through the pathless fields of light,
When suddenly a change was wrought, and *I was clothed in White.*
We stood before a City's walls, most glorious to behold;
We pass'd through gates of glistening pearl, o'er streets of purest gold;
It needed not the sun by day, the silver moon by night;
The glory of the LORD was there, the LAMB Himself its light.
Bright angels paced the shining streets, sweet music fill'd the air,
And white-robed saints with glittering crowns, from every clime, were there;
And some that I had loved on earth stood with them round the throne,
'All worthy is the LAMB,' they sang, 'the glory His alone.'
But fairer far than all beside, I saw my SAVIOUR'S face;
And as I gazed He smiled on me with wondrous love and grace.
Lowly I bow'd before His throne, o'erjoyed that I at last

THE STARLESS CROWN.

Had gained the object of my hopes—that
    earth at length was past.
And then, in solemn tones, He said, 'Where
    is the diadem
That ought to sparkle on thy brow—adorn'd
    with many a gem?
I know thou hast believed on Me, and life
    through Me is thine;
But where are all those radiant stars that in
    thy crown should shine?
Yonder thou seest a glorious throng, and stars
    on every brow;
For every soul they led to Me they wear a jewel
    now!
And such *thy* bright reward had been if such
    had been thy *deed,*
If thou hadst sought some wand'ring feet in
    path of peace to lead.
I did not mean that thou shouldst tread the
    way of life *alone,*
But that the clear and shining light which
    round thy footsteps shone,
Should guide some other weary feet to My
    bright home of rest,
And thus in blessing those around, thou hadst
    thyself been blest.'

THE STARLESS CROWN.

* * * * *

The vision faded from my sight, the voice no longer spake,
A spell seem'd brooding o'er my soul which long I fear'd to break,
And when at last I gazed around in morning's glimmering light,
My spirit fell o'erwhelmed beneath that vision's awful might.
I rose, and wept with chasten'd joy that yet I dwelt below,
That yet another hour was mine my faith by works to show;
That yet some sinner I might tell of JESUS' dying love,
And help to lead some weary soul to seek a home above.
And now, while on the earth I stay, my motto this shall be,
'To live no longer to myself, but Him who died for me!'
And graven on my inmost soul this word of truth divine,
'They that turn many to the Lord, bright as the stars shall shine.'

The Prayer of the Bereaved.

AVIOUR, whose crown'd humanity
    Still stoops to wipe the tearful eye,
Unto whose ear the voiceless sigh
        Pleads not in vain.
Thou who the broken heart hath heal'd,
Look on the woe to Thee reveal'd,
The burning fount of tears unseal'd,
        This bitter pain.

If blindly on a mortal head,
With lavish hand, I fondly shed
Gifts on Thy shrine more fitly laid,
        SAVIOUR, forgive!
With earthly love compelled to part,
Stricken by sorrow's keenest dart,
Have mercy on this wounded heart,
        And healing give.

If mortal accents all too dear,
With their deep music filled my ear,
So that Thy voice I failed to hear,
        O CHRIST, forgive!
Turn not this human heart to stone,
But once again with magic tone,
Thrill through its chambers dark and lone,
        Bidding it live.

If I have made a mortal eye
The star of my idolatry,
In whose dear light I hoped to die,
        Or longed to live—

THE PRAYER OF THE BEREAVED.

If one lov'd image ever seen
Thy glory and my soul between,
Forbade my trust on Thee to lean—
    JESUS, forgive!
For Thou for man didst bend the knee,
Anguish'd, in dark Gethsemane,
Nor scorn'd, in Thine extremity,
    A servant's aid;
And on our dreariest wastes below
Thy human footprints left, to show
That every storm of mortal woe
    Broke o'er Thy head.
Touched with our infirmity,
Rich in all human sympathy,
Brother of our humanity,
    Oh, Royal Priest!
This heart I on Thine altar lay,
A bleeding sacrifice to-day,
And from its quiv'ring depth, I pray,
    Be Thou my rest.
Sustain the trembling soul that dies,
Raise to Thyself these dreaming eyes,
And to its home within the skies
    Call back my love.
Anchor my hope within the vail,
That when this flesh and heart shall fail,
I may with joy Thy summons hail
    To Heaven above.
       I. L. BIRD.

The Best Position.

BENEATH the Cross of JESUS
    I lay me down to weep,
    And ponder o'er the matchless grace
Display'd on Calvary's steep.
(Isa. liii. 5, 6.)

Beneath the Cross of JESUS
    I lay me down to pray;
Nor look in vain for blessing
    In GOD's appointed way.
(Eph. i. 3.)

Beneath the Cross of JESUS
    I lay me down to hear
The welcome sound, ' 'Tis finished,'
    So sweet to sinner's ear.
(John xix. 30.)

Beneath the Cross of JESUS
    I lay me down to rest;
Here foolish doubts and anxious fears
    Are banish'd from my breast.
(Matt. xi. 28-30; John xiv. 1.)

THE BEST POSITION.

Beneath the Cross of JESUS
  I lay me down to love;
His blood the bond of union
  'Twixt saints below—above.
    (1 John iv. 19; John xv. 9.)

Beneath the Cross of JESUS
  I lay me down to feast,
On Him, my bleeding Sacrifice,
  My Altar, and my Priest.
    (John vi. 53-57.)

Beneath the Cross of JESUS
  I lay me down to sing,
'The grave has lost its victory,
  And death its venom'd sting.'
    (1 Cor. xv. 55-57.)

Beneath the Cross of JESUS
  I'd lay me down to die;
Till in the chariot of His love
  He bears me up on high.
    (John xiv. 3; John xvii. 24.)

Then seize my harp of gold,
  And tune it loud and long:
The Cross of JESUS crucified,
  My everlasting song.
    (Rev. v. 9, 10; Rev. xiv. 3. 4.)

Abide with Me.

'JESUS answered and said unto him, If any man love Me, he will keep My words: and My Father will love him, and We will come unto him, and make Our abode with him.'—JOHN xiv. 23.

BIDE with me! fast falls the even-tide:
　　The darkness deepens; LORD, with me
　　　　abide!
When other helpers fail, and comforts flee,
Help of the helpless, O abide with me!

Swift to its close ebbs out life's little day;
Earth's joys grow dim, its glories pass away;
Change and decay in all around I see:
O Thou, who changest not, abide with me!

Not a brief glance I beg, a passing word,
But, as Thou dwell'st with Thy disciples, LORD,
Familiar, condescending, patient, free;
Come not to sojourn, but abide, with me!

Come not in terrors, as the King of kings,
But in Thy grace, with healing in Thy wings;
Tears for all woes, a heart for every plea;
Come, Friend of sinners, thus abide with me!

ABIDE WITH ME.

Thou on my head in early youth didst smile,
And, tho' rebellious and perverse meanwhile,
Thou hast not left me, oft as I left Thee:
On to the close, O LORD, abide with me!

I need Thy Presence every passing hour—
What but Thy grace can foil the Tempter's
    power?
Who like Thyself my guide and stay can be?
Through cloud and sunshine, O abide with me!

I fear no foe, with Thee at hand to bless;
Ills have no weight, and tears no bitterness;
Where is death's sting? where, grave, thy vic-
    tory?
I triumph still if Thou abide with me!

Reveal Thyself before my closing eyes;
Shine through the gloom, and point me to the
    skies: [shadows flee:
Heaven's morning breaks, and earth's vain
In life, in death, O LORD, abide with me!

And when my soul, released from earth, shall
    soar   [more—
To realms of bliss, where I shall weep no
O wondrous thought! O glorious ecstasy!
For ever, LORD, I shall abide with THEE!   LYTE.

'Look Unto Me.'

Isaiah xlv. 22.

'The God of Salvation, and the God of Providence: therefore, as the God of Providence, look to Him to supply every want of "the life that now is;" as the God of Salvation, look to Him to save for eternity.'

Look unto Me, and be ye saved
    From all your depths of sin;
    From every crimson stain without,
And strongest power within.

Look unto Me, and be ye saved
    From all your earthly care;
Alike I grasp eternity,
    And number every hair.

Look unto Me, for I am God—
    To Me belongs all power,
At once to give *eternal* life,
    And guide each passing hour.

'LOOK UNTO ME!'

Look unto Me, and be ye saved
   From every doubt and fear;
Your warfare is accomplished,
   Your path to glory clear.

Look unto Me—'tis no great deed,
   A humble *look* to cast;
This is enough—the power that saves
   Is Mine, from first to last.

Look unto Me, while life endures,
   I give each fleeting breath;
Look unto Me, when death is nigh,
   I hold the keys of death.

Look unto Me, for I am God;
   Whate'er to Me is given,
Whate'er committed to My care,
   Is safe, for earth or heaven.

E. H. H.

Nature and Faith.

We wept—'twas *Nature* wept—but Faith
Can pierce beyond the gloom of death,
And in yon world, so fair and bright,
Behold thee in refulgent light!
We miss thee here, yet *Faith* would rather
Know thou art with thy Heavenly Father.
  Nature sees the body dead—
  Faith beholds the spirit fled;
Nature stops at Jordan's tide—
Faith beholds the other side;
That, but hears farewell, and sighs—
This, thy welcome in the skies;
Nature mourns a *cruel* blow—
Faith assures it is not so;
Nature never sees thee more—
Faith but sees thee gone before;
Nature tells a dismal story—
Faith has visions full of glory;
Nature views the change with sadness—
Faith contemplates it with gladness;

NATURE AND FAITH.

Nature murmurs—*Faith* gives meekness,
' Strength is perfected in weakness ; '
Nature writhes, and hates the rod—
Faith looks up, and blesses GOD ;
Sense looks downwards—*Faith* above ;
That sees harshness—*this* sees love.
Oh! let *Faith* victorious be—
Let it reign triumphantly!
But thou art gone! not lost, but flown ;
Shall I then ask thee back, my own?
Back—and leave thy spirit's brightness?
Back—and leave thy robes of whiteness?
Back—and leave the Lamb who feeds thee?
Back—from founts to which He leads thee?
Back—and leave thy Heavenly Father?
Back—to earth and sin?—Nay, rather
Would I live in solitude!
I *would* not ask thee, if I *could* ;
But patient wait the high decree
That calls my spirit home to thee!

'We Would See Jesus.'

John xii. 21.

'We would see Jesus'—all is gloom around
    us, [gone by;
Dark shadows falling from the years
The sins of other days, like phantoms rising,
Lifting their hands for judgment to the sky.
Where shall we hide us from these pale ac-
    cusers?
How shall we answer to the judgment call?
O for *one* sight of *Him*, our own Redeemer,
Bearing *our* guilt, paying our ransom—all!

'We would see Jesus'—we are worn and weary
Beneath the heat and burden of the day;
Each with his load of care, or toil, or sorrow,
Ready to faint and falter by the way.
Yet in the very path which we are treading
On earth, O Lord, we know Thyself hast gone;
O to behold Thee *there*, our Friend and Brother!
Guiding and guarding, as we journey on.

'We would see Jesus'—dearest ties are break-
    ing,
Lovely and loving ones have left our side;

'WE WOULD SEE JESUS.'

Is there one bond which death will not dis-
    sever,   [divide?
One Friend from whom the grave will not
There is! there is! the LORD of Life remaineth
The same to-day as He hath been of yore;
And Faith, the everlasting Friend beholding,
Can part from all beside, and weep no more.

'We would see JESUS'—nearer and still nearer
Come the dark valley and the lonely tomb;
Who shall uphold us on that unknown journey?
What star of hope shall light us through the
    gloom?
O CHRIST, forsake us not! Thou dost remember
Thy mortal anguish on Thy heavenly throne;
Reveal Thyself, when earth is disappearing—
Come in the hour of need, and save Thine own.

'We would see JESUS'—O that blissful vision
Is all we ask to bid our fears depart!
So shall we hasten on, in shade and sunshine,
With step unwearied and unshrinking heart.
Abide with us, good LORD!—the evening closes;
No longer leave us, till the shadows flee,
Till the bright morning dawn, when Thou
    shalt call us
For ever, where Thou art, to dwell with Thee.

I am the Shepherd True.

(FOUND IN THE POCKET OF A PRIEST.) *Faber*

I was wandering and weary
    When the Saviour came unto me,
  For the paths of sin were dreary,
And the world had ceased to woo me;
And I thought I heard Him say,
As He came along His way—
  'Wandering souls, O do come near me;
  My sheep should never fear Me,
    I am the Shepherd true.'

At first I would not hearken,
  But put off till the morrow;
But life began to darken,
  And I was sick with sorrow;
And I thought I heard Him say,
As He came along His way—
  'Wandering souls, O do come near Me;
  My sheep should never fear Me,
    I am the Shepherd true.'

At last I stopped to listen
  (*His* voice could ne'er deceive me),
I saw His kind eye glisten,
  So anxious to relieve me;

I AM THE SHEPHERD TRUE.

And I was sure I heard Him say,
As He came along His way—
  'Wandering souls, O do come near Me;
  My sheep should never fear Me,
    I am the Shepherd true.'

He took me on His shoulder,
    And tenderly He kissed me;
He bade my love grow bolder;
    And said how He had missed me;
And I was sure I heard Him say,
As He went along His way—
  'Wandering souls, O do come near Me;
  My sheep should never fear Me,
    I am the Shepherd true.'

I thought His love would weaken
    As more and more He knew me;
But it burneth like a beacon,
    And its light and heat go through me;
And I ever hear Him say,
As He goes along His way,—
  'Wandering souls, O do come near Me;
  My sheep should never fear Me,
    I am the Shepherd true.'

I Will Bless Thee.

'I WILL bless the Lord at all times.'—PSALM xxxiv. 1.

WILL bless Thee—for seasons of gladness,
    When Thou madest my cup to run
      o'er;
I will bless Thee—for dark days of sadness;
    For *these*, LORD, I bless Thee still more.

The seasons of gladness—they taught me
    How ready my heart was to stray:
The dark days of sadness—they brought me
    To Thee, as my one only stay.

I bless Thee—for friends Thou didst give me,
    Whose kindness oft soften'd my care:
I thought that they never would leave me
    All lonely and desolate here.

My frail gourds they quickly did wither,
    And I sank 'neath the scorching wind's blast,
When Thy pitiful voice said, 'Come hither;
    My wings over thee I will cast.'

I bless Thee—for these times of trial,
    Which taught me my rest was not here;
And that Thou, in Thy heavenly vial,
    Hast promised to treasure each tear.

I WILL BLESS THEE.

I have blessed Thee—when this heart was aching
  With wounds which Thou only didst know:
I have blessed Thee—when all seemed forsaking
  The weary one, steep'd in her woe.

I bless Thee, my Lord, for the hours
  Of lonely communion with Thee;
For the world, with all its bright flowers,
  Never brought so much sweetness to me.

I bless Thee, my Lord, for Thy dealings—
  The darkest—now brightest to me;
For they wean'd me from earth, and its feelings,
  And they taught me my peace is in Thee.

And now, for the bright hope of glory,
  I will bless Thee, O Lord, day by day;
But should I be left till I'm hoary,
  I know Thou wilt still be my stay.

And when to Thy home Thou hast brought me,
  How I'll bless Thee for ALL Thy great love;
How I'll praise Thee, my Saviour, who bought me,
  And still keeps me by grace from above!

C.H.I.

Nothing Between.

Nothing between, Lord, nothing between,
    Let me Thy glory see,
   Draw my soul close to Thee,
   Then speak in love to me,
             Nothing between.

Nothing between, Lord, nothing between,
    Let not earth's din and noise
   Stifle Thy still small voice;
   In it let me rejoice,
             Nothing between.

Nothing between, Lord, nothing between,
    Nothing of earthly care,
   Nothing of tear or prayer,
   No robe that self may wear,
             Nothing between.

Nothing between, Lord, nothing between,
    Unbelief disappear,
   Vanish each doubt and fear,
   Fading when Thou art near,
             Nothing between.

NOTHING BETWEEN.

Nothing between, Lord, nothing between,
    Shine with unclouded ray,
    Chasing each mist away,
    O'er my whole heart bear sway,
            Nothing between.

Nothing between, Lord, nothing between,
    Thus may I walk with Thee,
    Thee only may I see,
    Thine only let me be,
            Nothing between.

Nothing between, Lord, nothing between,
    Till Thine eternal light,
    Rising on earth's dark night,
    Bursts on my open sight,
            Nothing between.

Nothing between, Lord, nothing between,
    Till, the last conflict o'er,
    I stand on Canaan's shore
    With Thee for evermore,
            Nothing between.

                    E. H. H.

'That Rock is Christ.'

Y hope is built on nothing less
Than JESUS' Blood and Righteousness;
I dare not trust the sweetest frame,
But wholly lean on JESUS' Name.
  On CHRIST, the Solid Rock, I stand,
  All other ground is sinking sand.

When darkness veils His lovely face,
I rest on His unchanging grace;
In every high and stormy gale,
My anchor holds within the vail.
  On CHRIST, the solid Rock, I stand,
  All other ground is sinking sand.

His Oath, His Covenant, and Blood,
Support me in the sinking flood;
When every earthly prop gives way,
He then is all my hope and stay.
  On CHRIST, the solid Rock, I stand,
  All other ground is sinking sand.

When I shall launch to worlds unseen,
O may I then be found in Him,
Drest in His Righteousness alone,
Faultless to stand before the Throne!
  On CHRIST, the solid Rock, I stand,
  All other ground is sinking sand,
       REES.

Coming!

'WHAT I say unto you I say unto all, Watch.'—MARK xiii. 37.

'At even, or at midnight, or at the cock-crowing, or in the morning.'

' T may be in the evening,
    When the work of the day is done,
And you have time to sit in the twilight
    And watch the sinking sun,
While the long bright day dies slowly
    Over the sea,
And the hour grows quiet and holy
    With thoughts of Me,
While you hear the village children
    Passing along the street,
Among those thronging footsteps
    May come the sound of MY FEET:
Therefore I tell you, Watch!
    By the light of the evening star,
When the room is growing dusky
    As the clouds afar;
Let the door be on the latch
    In your home,
For it may be through the gloaming
    I will come.

COMING!

'It may be when the midnight
    Is heavy upon the land,
And the black waves lying dumbly
    Along the sand;
When the moonless night draws close,
And the lights are out in the house;
    When the fires burn low and red,
And the watch is ticking loudly
    Beside the bed:
Though you sleep, tired out, on your
        couch,
Still your heart must wake and watch
    In the dark room,
For it may be at midnight
    I will come.

'It may be at the cock-crow,
When the night is dying slowly
    In the sky,
And the sea looks calm and holy,
Waiting for the dawn of the golden sun
    Which draweth nigh;
When the mists are on the valleys, shading
    The rivers chill,
And My morning star is fading, fading
    Over the hill:
Behold I say unto you, Watch!

COMING!

Let the door be on the latch
    In your home;
In the chill before the dawning,
Between the night and morning
    I may come.

' It may be in the morning,
    When the sun is bright and strong,
And the dew is glittering sharply
    Over the little lawn;
When the waves are laughing loudly
    Along the shore,
And the little birds are singing sweetly
    About the door.
With the long day's work before you,
    You rise up with the sun,
And the neighbours come in to talk a little
    Of all that must be done;
But remember that I may be the next
    To come in at the door,
To call you from your busy work
    For evermore:
As you work your heart must watch,
For the door is on the latch
    In your room,
And it may be in the morning
    I will come.'

COMING!

So He passed down my cottage garden,
    By the path that leads to the sea,
Till He came to the turn of the little road,
    Where the birch and laburnum tree
Lean over and arch the way:
There I saw Him a moment stay,
    And turn once more to me,
    As I wept at the cottage door,
And lift up His hands in blessing—
    Then I saw His face no more.
And I stood still in the door-way,
    Leaning against the wall,
Not heeding the fair white roses,
    Though I crushed them, and let them fall,
Only looking down the pathway,
    And looking towards the sea,
And wondering, and wondering,
    When He would come back for me,
Till I was aware of an Angel,
    Who was going swiftly by,
With the gladness of one who goeth
    In the light of GOD Most High.
He passed the end of the cottage
    Towards the garden gate,
(I suppose he was come down,
At the setting of the sun,
To comfort some one in the village
    Whose dwelling was desolate,)
And he passed before the door
        Beside my place,

COMING!

And the likeness of a smile
    Was on his face :—
'Weep not,' he said, 'for unto you is given
    To watch for the coming of His feet,
Who is the Glory of our blessed Heaven;
    The work and watching will be very sweet
        Even in an earthly home,
And in such an hour as you think not
    He will come.'

So I am watching quietly
    Every day:
Whenever the sun shines brightly
    I rise and say,—
Surely it is the shining of His face!
And look unto the gates of His high place,
    Beyond the sea,
For I know He is coming shortly
    To summon me.
And when a shadow falls across the window
    Of my room,
Where I am working my appointed task,
I lift my head to watch the door and ask
    If He is come;
And the Angel answers sweetly,
    In my home,—
'Only a few more shadows,
    And He will come.'

                        B. M.

The Dying Christian Father.

'LET me die the death of the righteous, and let my last end be like his!'

My day is dippin' in the West, 'tis gloamin' wi' me noo,
I hear the sough o' Jordan's wave, that I maun travel through;
Yet 'tisna Jordan's wave I fear, nor tremble at the strife,
But, oh! this sunderin' o' hearts, this leavin' weans an' wife.

What though we ken o' better things, a fairer world abune, [follow sune;
Where lost frien's are awaiting us, an' a' maun
This rendin' o' the siller strings, that tether heart to heart—
Oh! it tries puir human nature sair, an' mak's us laith to pairt.

Gae rax me bye the Bible, wife, while yet I'm fit to see,
Ere death creep o'er my cauldrife back, an' flap my failin' e'e;
An' let us sing a pairtin' sang before we sunder'd be, [to dree.
For ye canna ha'e me lang noo, I ha'ena lang
There, pit the pillow to my back, an' ease me up awee, [faither dee;
An' bring them a' to my bedside to see their

THE DYING CHRISTIAN FATHER.

Noo, raise the Bible up a thocht, it's ower
    laigh on my knee;
An' shift the licht a kennin back, it's ower
    strong for my e'e.—

He waled, he sang the pairtin' sang—his
    voice was firm an' clear—
An' read the fourteenth o' St John, nor did
    he shed a tear:
Sae is it wi' the man o' God, when life's day's
    wark is dune,
Nae future fears disturb his mind, nae ruefu'
    looks behin'.—

O! but it gaes me great relief, the singin' o'
    that sang;
My clay is crumbling fast awa, my spirit noo
    grows strang:
My wife, my weans, we a' maun pairt, sae
    dinna sab sae sair,
But dicht the tears frae aff your face, an' let
    us join in prayer.

An' let us join in prayer to Him that's wantin'
    me awa,
That He may be a faithfu' Frien' an' Faither
    to ye a'.—
He turned his glaizin' e'e to heaven, and raised
    his wither'd hand:
Noo, safely through cauld Jordan's wave, he
    reach'd the better land.

'The Everlasting Arms.'

Deut. xxxiii. 27.

PILGRIMS on the road to glory,
 Pressing to the heavenly prize,
  'Mid the ills that now annoy you,
 'Mid the dangers that arise;
When your way is dark and dreary,
 Rugged, fill'd with rude alarms,
When perplex'd, exhausted, weary,
 Trust the '*Everlasting Arms.*'

When the waves of trouble heighten,
 When the billows fiercely foam,
All you see conspires to frighten,
 Friends and helpers fail to come;
When of human aid despairing,
 And no voice the tempest calms,
Think of this, that underneath you
 Are the '*Everlasting Arms.*'

'THE EVERLASTING ARMS.'

When corroding cares oppress you,
   When the tempter's darts assail,
When your inbred foes distress you,
   When they threaten to prevail;
When you dread the thought of yielding,
   When you feel to die is gain,
When your hope seems just expiring,
   '*Everlasting Arms*' sustain.

And when all below is closing,
   When you touch the chilling flood,
When you feel the waters rising,
   You shall find the promise good.
Timid Christians, venture on it,
   Bid farewell to all alarms;
'Tis enough that *underneath you*
   Are the '*Everlasting Arms.*'

My Ain Countree.

I AM far frae my hame, and I'm weary oftenwhiles
    For the langed-for hame-bringing, an' my FATHER's welcome smiles;
I'll ne'er be fu' content, until my een do see
The gowden gates o' heaven, an' my ain countree.

The earth is fleck'd wi' flow'rs, mony tinted, fresh, and gay,
The birdies warble blithely, for my FATHER made them sae;
But these sichts an' these soun's will as naething be to me,
When I hear the angels singing in my ain countree.

I've His gude word of promise, that some gladsome day the KING
To his ain royal Palace His banished hame will bring;
Wi' een an' wi' hearts running owre we shall [see
'The King in His beauty,' an' our ain countree.

My sins hae been mony, an' my sorrows hae been sair,   [ber'd mair:
But there they'll never vex me, nor be remem-

MY AIN COUNTREE.

His Bluid hath made me white, *His* hand shall
    dry mine e'e,
When He brings me hame at last to my ain
    countree.

Like a bairn to its mither, a wee birdie to its
    nest,   [breast;
I wad fain be ganging noo unto my SAVIOUR'S
For He gathers in His bosom witless, worth-
    less lambs, like me,
An' carries them Himself to His ain countree.

He's faithfu' that hath promised, He'll surely
    come again,
He'll keep His tryst wi' me, at what hour I
    dinna ken;
But He bids me still to watch, an' ready aye
    to be
To gang at ony moment to my ain countree.

So I'm watching aye an' singing o' my Hame
    as I wait,
For the soun'ing o' His footfa' this side the
    gowden gate:
GOD gie His grace to ilka ane wha listens noo
    to me,
That we may a' gang in gladness to our ain
    countree.

The Cancelled Bond.

He gave me back the bond,—
    It was a heavy debt,—
And as He gave, He smiled, and said,
  '*Thou wilt not* Me *forget.*'

He gave me back the bond,—
    The seal was torn away,—
And as He gave, He smiled, and said,
  '*Think thou of* Me *alway.*'

That bond I still will keep,
    Although it cancell'd be;
It tells me what I owe to Him
    Who paid the debt for me.

I look on it and smile,
    I look again and weep;
This record of His love to me
    For ever will I keep.

A *bond* it is no more,
    But it shall ever tell,
That all I owed was fully paid
    By my Emmanuel.

A Something to All.

We a' hae a something, be't great or be't sma',   [to a';
  To rich and to puir, there's a something
Yer gear may be rife, or yer gear may be scant,   [could want.
  Ye'll aye hae a something ye'll think ye

It's whiles a bit thing, mair bother than grief,
Like a jag i' the thoom, or a seed i' the teeth:
And whiles it's a something o' sorrow and care,   [hair.
  That wearies the speerit, and whitens the

But tho' ye be weary—tho' sair and unseen
The saut silent tears fa' like peas frae yer e'en,—   [swerve;
Be still, and frae virtue and faith dinna
  Yer something has some hidden purpose to serve.

Then bear wi' yer something, whatever it be,
Wi' the courage that Heaven's aye waiting to gie;   [men—
And think o' His words to the children o'
  'What ye dinna ken here, ye hereafter shall ken.'
                                  W.

Divine Guidance.

Isaiah xlii. 16.

ORTH into the darkness passing,
　　Nothing can I hear or see,
　Save the Hand outstretch'd to guide me,
　　And the Voice that calls to me:
'I will bring the blind by pathways
　　That they know not, nor have known'—
'Tis a way untried, untrodden,
　　But I shall not walk alone.

HE who leads me knows the pathway;
　　Every step Himself has plann'd,
Sees the end from the beginning—
　　Let me only feel His Hand,
I will walk into the darkness,
　　Shrink not, but with patience wait:
'Darkness shall be light before them,
　　And the crooked shall be straight.'

Yet I tremble! lest there meet me
　　Sorrows, foes, I ne'er have known,
When, to God my hands outstretching,
　　I may find myself ALONE!—
Listen—'I WILL NOT FORSAKE THEM!'
　　Then I need no evil fear:
E'en though shades of death should gather,
　　All is well, if THOU art near.

DIVINE GUIDANCE.

Guidance, Light, and Presence promis'd,
   Lord, Thou couldst not give me more!
Thus the mystic fiery pillar
   Mov'd the chosen tribes before;
Redden'd far the sandy desert
   Through the silence of the night—
Symbol of a Guard unsleeping,—
   Turning darkness into light.

Lead the way, then, where Thou pleasest,
   Only keep me close to Thee,
Craving not to see the distant,
   Well content that *Thou* dost see.
Have I not my all committed
   To Thy keeping long ago?
Knowing Him whom I have trusted,
   More I do not need to know.

Teach me still Thy priceless lesson,
   'Walk by faith and not by sight'—
Give a childlike heart, to trust Thee,
   Waiting for the perfect light.
Every step in all the journey
   Shall reveal Thy care and love,
When with open'd eyes I trace it
   From the radiant heights above.

                                  H. A. B.

The Christian's Hope.

'CHRIST in you the hope of glory.'—COL. i. 27.
'Which hope we have as an anchor of the soul, both sure and stedfast, and which entereth into that within the veil.'—HEB. vi. 19.

'MIDST changing scenes, and changing friends,
 There is one blessed hope,
Which cheers the weary on their way,
 And lifts the fainting up.

CHRIST is that hope—the sinner's stay,
 Where I for refuge flee :
This all my claim, this all my boast,
 That He has died for me.

Dark storms may come, rough winds may blow,
 My anchor will not move ;
Temptation's waves may foam around,
 I'm safe, kept by His love.

While JESUS lives, and JESUS loves,
 Surrounded by His arm,
Not all the powers of earth or hell
 Can do His feeblest harm.

While there I cling, His truth, His power,
 Shall be my strength and shield ;
However great the conflict be,
 He will not let me yield.

THE CHRISTIAN'S HOPE.

My anchor's now within the vail,
  For me, He lives above;
And He has bound my life to His
  With strongest chains of love.

Shall, then, the world have charms for me,
  Which honours not my LORD?
Or shall I to its ways conform,
  Forbidden by His word?

No, gracious LORD; on things unseen—
  The glorious Home above!
The resting place for weary hearts,
  Whence they shall ne'er remove;

There, by Thy SPIRIT's mighty power,
  Be my affections stayed;
And may there be on all I do
  A heavenly impress made.

My business here, O let it be
  To glorify Thy name;
And try to win whoe'er I can,
  That they may do the same.

JESUS, my Anchor, Refuge, Hope,
  My Saviour and my King;
Through all life's dark and stormy waves,
  To Thee, to Thee, I cling.   C.H.I.

The Bible.

[THE following stanzas were composed by a convert from Popery, under the care of the Priest's Protection Society, Dublin. He wrote them in affliction, over the source from which he derived all his consolation—the Book of books.]

HAT book is that, whose page divine
Bears God's impress on every line,
And in man's soul makes light to shine?
                        The Bible.

When sin and sorrow, want and woe,
Assail poor mortals here below,
What book can them true comfort show?
                        The Bible.

What paints the beautiful and true,
And mirrors at a single view
The paths which here we should pursue?
                        The Bible.

What is the brightest gift the Lord,
In His great mercy, did award
To man, to be his shield and guard?
                        The Bible.

THE BIBLE.

What teaches love, and truth, and peace,
And bids goodwill 'mong men increase,
And bids strife, war, and murder cease?
The Bible.

What elevates and purifies
The souls of men, until they rise
Like brilliant stars set in the skies?
The Bible.

Oh! what can make this world of woe
With peace, and truth, and virtue glow,
Till man no sin or sorrow know?
The Bible.

What could our Emerald Isle restore
To that proud title which she bore,
Before popes' legates touch'd her shore?
The Bible.

What could the greatest blessing be
To banish Erin's ills, and free
Her sons from crime and misery?
The Bible.

THE BIBLE.

What gave to England her great name,
And o'er the earth spread Scotland's fame,
While Ireland naught but tears can claim?
      The Bible.

When error fled before its foes,
And Luther, like the morning, rose,
With what did he Rome's crimes expose?
      The Bible.

What is it now that baffles Rome,
Where error long has found a home,
In many a pagan pile and dome?
      The Bible.

What gives to man the power and will,
God's high behests to do—fulfil,
And points the way to Zion's hill?
      The Bible.

When death comes knocking at the door
And man's short life on earth is o'er,
What tells of bliss for evermore?
      The Bible.

The Changed Cross.

T was a time of sadness, and my heart,
Although it knew and loved the better
part,
Felt wearied with the conflict and the strife,
And all the needful discipline of life.

And while I thought on these, as given to me
My trial tests of faith and love to be,
It seemed as if I never could be sure
That faithful to the end I should endure.

And thus, no longer trusting to His might
Who says, 'We walk by faith and not by sight,'
Doubting—and almost yielding to despair,—
The thought arose, *My cross I cannot bear!*

Far heavier its weight must surely be,
Than those of others which I daily see;
Oh, if I might another burden choose,
Methinks I should not fear my crown to lose.

A solemn silence reigned on all around,
E'en Nature's voices uttered not a sound;
The evening shadows seemed of peace to tell,
And sleep upon my weary spirit fell.

THE CHANGED CROSS.

A moment's pause, and then a heavenly light
Beamed full upon my wondering, raptur'd sight;
Angels on silvery wings seemed every where,
And angels' music thrill'd the balmy air.

Then One, more fair than all the rest to see,
One, to whom all the others bowed the knee,
Came gently to me, as I trembling lay,
And 'Follow Me,' He said, 'I am the Way.'

Then, speaking thus, He led me far above,
And there, beneath a canopy of love,
Crosses of divers shape and size were seen,
Larger and smaller than mine own had been.

And one there was, most beauteous to behold,
A little one, with jewels set in gold—
Ah! this, methought, I can with comfort wear,
For it will be an easy one to bear.

And so the little cross I quickly took,
But all at once my frame beneath it shook;
The sparkling jewels, fair were they to *see*,
But far too heavy was their *weight* for me.

This may not be, I cried; and looked again
To see if any there could ease my pain,
But, one by one, I passed them slowly by,
Till on a lovely one I cast my eye.

THE CHANGED CROSS.

Fair flowers around its sculptur'd form entwin'd,
And grace and beauty seem'd in it combined;
Wondering, I gazed, and still I wondered more,
To think so many should have pass'd it o'er.

But, oh! that form so beautiful to see,
Soon made its hidden sorrows known to me;—
Thorns lay beneath those flowers and colours fair—
Sorrowing, I said, This cross I may not bear.

And so it was with each and all around,
Not one to suit my *need* could there be found;
Weeping, I laid each heavy burden down,
As my Guide gently said, 'No cross—no crown.'

At length to Him I raised my sadden'd heart;
He knew its sorrows, bid its doubts depart,—
'Be not afraid,' He said, 'but trust in Me,
'My perfect love shall now be shown to thee.'

And then, with lighten'd eyes and willing feet,
Again I turned my earthly cross to meet;
With forward footsteps turning not aside,
For fear some hidden evil might betide.

THE CHANGED CROSS.

And there, in the prepar'd appointed way,
Listening to hear, and ready to obey,
A cross I quickly found of plainest form,
With only words of love inscribed thereon.

With thankfulness I raised it from the rest,
And joyfully acknowledged it the best;
The *only* one of all the many there,
That I could feel was *good* for me to bear.

And while I thus my chosen one confess'd,
I saw a heavenly brightness on it rest,
And as I bent, my burden to sustain,
I recognised my own old cross again!

But, oh! how different did it seem to be,
Now I had learned its preciousness to see;
No longer could I unbelieving say—
Perhaps another is a better way.

Ah! no; henceforth my one desire shall be,
That He who knows me best should choose
    for me;
And so, whate'er His love sees good to send,
I'll trust it's best—because He knows the
    end.

L. P. W.

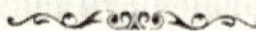

Sabbath Hymn for a Sick-room.

THOUSANDS, O LORD of hosts! to-day
    Around Thine altar meet;
    And tens of thousands throng to pay
Their homage at Thy feet.

They see Thy power and glory there,
    Where I have seen them too;
They read, they hear, they join in prayer,
    As I was wont to do.

They sing Thy deeds, as I have sung,
    In sweet and solemn lays:
Were I among them, my glad tongue
    Might learn new themes of praise.

For Thou art in their midst to teach,
    When on Thy name they call;
And Thou hast blessings, LORD, for each—
    Hast blessings, LORD, for all.

I, of such privilege bereft,
    In spirit turn to Thee;
Oh! hast Thou not a blessing left—
    A blessing, LORD, for me?

SABBATH HYMN FOR A SICK-ROOM.

The dew lies thick on all the ground,
  Shall my poor fleece be dry?
The manna rains from heaven around,
  Shall I of hunger die?

Behold Thy prisoner! loose my bands,
  If 'tis Thy gracious will;
If not, contented in Thine hands,
  Behold Thy pris'ner still.

I may not to Thy courts repair,
  Yet here Thou surely art;
Then consecrate a house of prayer
  In my surrender'd heart.

To Faith reveal the things unseen,
  To Hope the joys unfold;
Let Love, without a veil between,
  The glory *now* behold.

Lord Jesus, help me now to flee,
  And seek my hope alone in Thee;
Apply Thy Blood, Thy Spirit give,
  Subdue my sin, and let me live.

Lord! make Thy face on me to shine,
  That doubt and fear may cease;
Lift up Thy countenance benign
  On me, and give me peace.

The Blessed Dead.

'Blessed are the dead which die in the Lord.'—Rev. xiv. 13.

'I would not have you to be ignorant concerning them which are asleep, that ye sorrow not, even as others which have no hope. For if we believe that Jesus died and rose again, even so them also which sleep in Jesus will God bring with Him.'—1 Thess. iv. 13, 14.

H! weep not for the blessed dead,
　　Their days of grief are o'er ;
Their sicknesses, their pangs of heart,
　Are felt by them no more.

Oh ! weep not for the blessed dead,
　Their sins are all forgiven !
Through Him who wash'd them in His blood,
　And made them meet for Heaven.

Oh ! weep not for the blessed dead,
　No tears their eyes bedim ;
They see His face, who, by His grace,
　Had turned their hearts to Him.

THE BLESSED DEAD.

Oh! weep not for the blessed dead,
    They are but gone before;
Their schooling days of pain are past,
    And ours will soon be o'er.

Oh! weep not for the blessed dead,
    Safe in their Father's Home;
They've gained the victory over death,
    And triumph'd o'er the tomb.

Oh! weep not for the blessed dead,
    Their struggles all are o'er;
They live with Him, who gave them life,
    And they shall die no more!

Oh! weep not for the blessed dead,
    As hopeless mourners may;
For soon His sleeping ones He'll bring,
    And take His saints away.

Oh! weep not for the blessed dead,
    We are but strangers here;
And though so weary oft with woe,
    Our Home we're drawing near.

THE BLESSED DEAD.

Oh! weep not for the blessed dead,
  They have eternal rest;
Where no harsh sounds are ever heard,
  Nor earthly cares molest.

Oh! weep not for the blessed dead,
  Nor wish them here again:
What! bring them back to earth and sin,
  To feel its grief and pain!

Oh! weep not for the blessed dead,
  They would not change with thee,
Nor have their spirits bound again,
  Now happy, pure, and free.

Oh! weep not for the blessed dead,
  But try to catch their strain,
While on their golden harps they sing
  His love, for sinners slain.

Oh! weep not for the blessed dead,
  Yonder in robes of white!
Made perfect through the LAMB OF GOD,
  They shine in glorious light.   C. H. I.

What Think ye of Christ?

MATT. xxii. 42.

HAT think you of Christ? is the test
    To try both your state and your scheme;
You cannot be right in the rest,
    Unless you think rightly of Him.
As Jesus appears in your view,
    As He is belovéd or not;
So God is disposéd to you,
    And mercy or wrath are your lot.

Some take Him a creature to be,
    A man, or an angel at most;
Sure these have not feelings like me,
    Nor know themselves wretched and lost.
So guilty, so helpless, am I,
    I durst not confide in His blood,
Nor on His protection rely,
    Unless I were sure He is God.

Some call Him a Saviour in word,
    But mix their own works with His plan;
And hope He His help will afford,
    When they have done all that they can.

WHAT THINK YE OF CHRIST?

If doings prove rather too light
   (A little, they own, they may fail),
They purpose to make up full weight,
   By casting His Name in the scale.

Some style Him the Pearl of great price,
   And say, He's the Fountain of joys,
Yet feed upon folly and vice,
   And cleave to the world and its toys.
Like Judas, the SAVIOUR they kiss,
   And while they salute Him, betray;
Ah! what will profession like this
   Avail in His terrible day?

If ask'd what of JESUS I think?
   Though still my best thoughts are but poor,
I say, He's my Meat and my Drink,
   My Life, and my Strength, and my Store:
My Shepherd, my Husband, my Friend,
   My SAVIOUR from sin and from thrall;
My Hope from beginning to end,
   My Portion, my LORD, and my All.

NEWTON.

'If you Love Me, Lean Hard.'

[MISS FISKE, who has laboured so long and successfully amongst the Persian women, says, that as she was one Sunday sitting, faint and weary, on a mat on the ground, during Divine service, and was longing for rest, a woman came and placed herself behind her, so as to support her; and on Miss Fiske's declining to lean upon her, she drew her back, and said, 'If you love me, *lean hard.*' Then came the Master's voice, repeating, 'If you love Me, *lean hard.*' Thus body and soul found support and refreshment.]

Softly and gently these words were breathed
   To the loved one thus first address'd,
As she sat on the ground, in a far off land,
   Whilst her weary worn frame craved rest.

The Persian offers her firm, strong form,
   As a living prop and stay,
But the pressure so light shows that she who leans,
Fears lest she too heavily weigh.

Love wants the whole burden upon herself cast,
   And deems it a joy to bear;

'IF YOU LOVE ME, LEAN HARD.'

'If indeed, then, you love me, lean hard, oh!
    lean hard,'
  Is her tender importunate prayer.

And the HOLY COMFORTER echoed the words,
  In the depths of the fainting one's soul;
And she felt that her SAVIOUR's love required
  All her care she should on Him roll.

And thus while the body support and stay
  Found by leaning in trustful love,
The soul, in its weakness, was learning to rest
  On the unseen, but strong Friend above.

My SAVIOUR, these words bring a lesson from
    Thee;
  For, alas! I as yet but *half* trust;
I know not what 'tis to *take hold of Thy*
    strength,
  Thus often fall prone in the dust.

Yet He who has borne the dread load of my
    sins,
  Will surely my weaknesses bear;
He who takes up the isles as a very small
    thing,
  Cannot sink 'neath the load of my care.

'IF YOU LOVE ME, LEAN HARD.'

He has carried my sorrows, and borne all
    my griefs,
  And still is almighty to save;
That my weakness should rest on His infinite
    strength,
  Surely well from His child He may crave.

He bids me to lean my soul *wholly* on Him,
  For without Him I tremble and fall;
And with deep thankful joy, I obey and
    respond
  To His loving, compassionate call.

In quiet repose, like a babe on the breast,
  Would I rest, gracious SAVIOUR, on Thee:
I am weakness itself, but Thou, Thou art my
    strength,—
  Thy arms everlasting clasp me.

Oh! teach me at all times on Thee to lean
    hard,
  And show thus how truly I love;
Keep me close to Thyself, ever bound to
    Thy side,
  Till I lean on Thy bosom above.

F. E. W.

Old Testament Gospel.

Israel, in ancient days,
   Not only had a view
  Of Sinai in a blaze,
But learn'd the Gospel too:
The types and figures were a glass
In which they saw a Saviour's face.

The paschal sacrifice
   And blood-besprinkled door,*
Seen with enlighten'd eyes,
   And once applied with power,
Would teach the need of other blood
To reconcile an angry God.

The Lamb, the Dove, set forth
   His perfect innocence,†
Whose blood, of matchless worth,
   Should be the soul's defence;
For He who can for sin atone
Must have no failings of His own.

* Exod. xii. 13.   † Lev. xii. 6.

OLD TESTAMENT GOSPEL.

The Scape-Goat, on his head,*
   The people's trespass bore,
And to the desert led,
   Was to be seen no more:
In him our Surety seem'd to say,
' Behold! I bear your sins away.'

Dipt in his fellow's blood,
   The living bird went free; †
The type, well understood,
   Express'd the sinner's plea:
Described a guilty soul enlarged,
And by a SAVIOUR's death discharged.

JESUS, I love to trace,
   Throughout the sacred page,
The footsteps of Thy grace,
   The same in every age!
O grant that I may faithful be
To clearer light vouchsafed to me!

COWPER.

---

*Lev. xvi. 21.   † Lev. xiv. 51-53.

Looking at the Cross.

In evil long I took delight,
    Unawed by shame or fear,
    Till a new object struck my sight,
And stopp'd my wild career.

I saw One hanging on a tree,
    In agonies and blood,
Who fix'd His languid eyes on me,
    As near His cross I stood.

Sure never till my latest breath
    Can I forget that look;
It seem'd to charge me with His death,
    Though not a word He spoke.

My conscience felt and own'd the guilt,
    And plunged me in despair;
I saw my sins His blood had spilt,
    And help'd to nail Him there.

LOOKING AT THE CROSS.

Alas! I knew not what I did;
    But now my tears are vain:
Where shall my trembling soul be hid,
    For I the Lord have slain?

A second look He gave, which said,
    'I freely all forgive;
This blood is for thy ransom paid—
    I die, that thou mayst live.'

Thus, while His death my sin displays
    In all its blackest hue,
(Such is the mystery of grace,)
    It seals my pardon too!

With pleasing grief and mournful joy
    My spirit now is fill'd,
That I should such a life destroy,
    Yet live by Him I kill'd!

NEWTON.

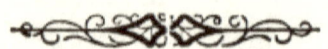

How the Lord Sustains.

'Cast thy burden upon the Lord, and He shall sustain thee.'

CHRISTIAN, when thy way seems darkest,
    When thine eyes with tears are dim,
Straight to God, thy Father, hast'ning,
    Tell thy troubles all to Him.
Not to human ear confiding
    Thy sad tale of grief and care;
But before thy Father kneeling,
    Pour out all thy sorrows there.

Sympathy of friends may cheer thee,
    When the fierce wild storm has burst:
But God only can console thee,
    When it breaks upon thee first;
Go with words, or tears, or silence,
    Only lay thee at His feet,
Thou shalt prove how great His pity,
    And His tenderness how sweet.

Think, too, thy Divine Redeemer
    Knew, as thou canst never know,
All the deepest depths of suffering,
    All the weight of human woe.
And though now in glory seated,
    He can hear thy feeblest cry,
Even hear the stifled sighing
    Of thy dumb heart's agony.

HOW THE LORD SUSTAINS.

All thy griefs by Him are order'd,
    Needful is each one for thee;
Every tear by Him is counted,
    One too much there cannot be;
And if, whilst they fall so thickly,
    Thou canst own His way is right,
Then each bitter tear of anguish
    Precious is in JESUS' sight.

Far too well thy SAVIOUR loves thee,
    To allow thy life to be
One lone, calm, unbroken summer,
    One unruffled, stormless sea.
He would have thee fondly nestling
    Closer to His loving breast;
He would have that world seem brighter
    Where alone is perfect rest.

Though His wise and loving purpose
    Clearly yet thou mayst not see,
Still believe, with faith unshaken,
    All will work for good to thee.
Therefore, when thy way is gloomy,
    And thine eyes with tears are dim,
Straight to GOD, thy Father, hast'ning,
    Tell thy sorrows all to Him.

C. FENN.

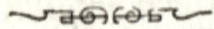

Morning Hymn.

Awake, my soul, and with the sun
Thy daily stage of duty run;
Shake off dull sloth, and joyful rise
To pay thy morning sacrifice.

Thy precious time misspent, redeem;
Each present day thy last esteem;
Improve thy talent with due care—
For the Great Day thyself prepare.

Let all thy converse be sincere,
Thy conscience as the noon-day clear;
For God's all-seeing eye surveys
Thy secret thoughts, and works, and ways.

Wake, and lift up thyself, my heart,
And with the angels bear thy part,
Who, day and night, unwearied sing
High praise to the Eternal King.

Lord, I my vows to Thee renew;
Scatter my sins as morning dew;
Guard my first springs of thought and will,
And with Thyself my spirit fill.

Direct, control, suggest this day,
All I design, or do, or say;
That all my powers, with all their might,
In Thy sole glory may unite. BP. KEN.

Evening Hymn.

LORY to Thee, my GOD, this night,
For all the blessings of the light;
Keep me, O keep me, King of kings,
Under Thy own almighty wings.

Forgive me, LORD, for Thy dear Son,
The ill that I this day have done,
That with the world, myself, and Thee,
I, ere I sleep, at peace may be.

Teach me to live—that I may dread
The grave as little as my bed;
Teach me to die—that so I may
Rise glorious at the awful day.

O may my soul on Thee repose,
And balmy sleep mine eyelids close—
Sleep that my frame shall vig'rous make,
To serve my GOD when I awake.

If in the night I sleepless lie,
My soul with heavenly thoughts supply;
Let no ill dreams disturb my rest,
No powers of darkness me molest.

Praise GOD, from whom all blessings flow;
Praise Him, all creatures here below;
Praise Him, above, ye heavenly host,
Praise FATHER, SON, and HOLY GHOST. BP. KEN.

'She is not Dead, but Sleepeth.'

LUKE vii. 52.

'But I would not have you to be ignorant, brethren, concerning them which are ASLEEP, that ye sorrow not, even as others which have no hope. For if we believe that Jesus died and rose again, even so them also which SLEEP IN JESUS will God bring with him.'—1 THESS. iv. 13, 14.

H! call it not death—it is life begun,
    For the waters are pass'd, the home is won;
The ransomed spirit hath reach'd the shore,
Where they weep, and suffer, and sin no more.
She is safe in her FATHER's house above,
In the place prepared by her SAVIOUR's love:
To depart from a world of sin and strife,
And to be with JESUS—yes,—this is *life*.

Oh! call it not death—'tis a holy sleep,
And the precious dust the LORD doth keep;
She shall wake again—and how satisfied
With the likeness of Him for her who died!
As He rose again, she shall also rise
From the quiet bed where now safe she lies.
Then cheer ye, fond mourners, who sadly weep,
For happy are they who in JESUS *sleep*.

'SHE IS NOT DEAD BUT SLEEPETH.'

Oh! call it not death—'Tis a glorious rest,
' Yea, saith the Spirit,' for all such are blest;
' They rest from their labours, their work is done,
The goal is attain'd, the weary race run.
The battle is fought—the struggle is o'er,
The crown now replaces the cross they bore,
The pilgrimage path shall no more be trod—
' A *rest* remains to the people of GOD.'

Oh! call it not death—it is true, indeed,
The soul from the shackles of earth is freed;
'Tis true, that dissolv'd is the house of clay,
And the spirit, unchain'd, hath pass'd away;
'Tis true, too, the lov'd one hath gone before,—
The home how darken'd, that knows her no more!
He chides not your grief, for JESUS, too, wept
O'er the grave where His Friend, a Laz'rus *slept*.

But call it not death—a few short days o'er,
Ye shall meet her in glory, to part no more;
What a 'blessed hope!' lo! CHRIST shall appear
For ' the restitution of all things' here,
Then (if not till then) ye'll see her again,
When brought by the LORD with His glorious train,
Those ' *sleeping* in JESUS' shall be restor'd,
' And so shall we ever be with the LORD.'

E. E. H.

Watch Thou in all Things.

Be PATIENT—life is very brief,
    It passes quickly by;
    And if it prove a troubled scene
  Beneath a stormy sky,
It is but like the shaded night
That brings a morn of radiance bright.

Be HOPEFUL—cheerful faith will bring
    A living joy to thee,
And make thy life a hymn of praise,
    From doubt and murmur free;
Whilst, like a sunbeam, thou wilt bless,
And bring to others happiness.

Be EARNEST—an immortal soul
    Should be a worker true;
Employ thy talents for thy GOD,
    And ever keep in view
The Judgment scene, the last great day,
When heaven and earth shall pass away.

WATCH THOU IN ALL THINGS.

Be HOLY—let not sin's dark stain
   Thy spirit's whiteness dim;
Keep close to JESUS 'mid the world,
   And trust alone in Him:
So 'midst thy business and thy rest
Thou will be comforted and blest.

Be PRAYERFUL—ask, and thou wilt have
   Strength equal to thy day;
Prayer clasps the Hand that guides the
     world,
   O make it then thy stay!
Ask largely, and thy GOD will be
A kindly Giver unto thee.

Be READY—many fall around;
   Our loved ones disappear:
We know not when our call may come,
   Nor should we wait in fear;
If ready, we can calmly rest—
Living or dying, we are blest.

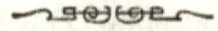

The Pilgrim.

THE CRY.

The way is dark, my FATHER! cloud on cloud
    Is gathering quickly o'er my head:
        and loud
The thunders roar above me. See, I stand
Like one bewildered; FATHER, take my hand,
        And through the gloom
        Lead safely home
               Thy child.

The day goes fast my FATHER; and the night
Is drawing darkly down. My faithless sight
Sees ghostly visions. Fears, a spectral band,
Encompass me. O FATHER! take my hand,
        And from the night
        Lead up to light
               Thy child.

The way is long, my FATHER! and my soul
Longs for the rest and quiet of the goal;
While yet I journey through this weary land,
Keep me from wand'ring. FATHER, take my hand,
        Quickly and straight
        Lead to Heaven's gate
               Thy child.

THE PILGRIM.

The path is rough, my FATHER! many a thorn
Has pierced me, and my weary feet are torn;
And bleeding marks the way. Yet thy command
    Bids me press forward. FATHER, take my hand;
             Then safe, and blest,
             Lead up to rest
                    Thy child.

The throng is great, my FATHER! many a doubt,
And fear, and danger, compass me about,
And foes oppress me sore. I cannot stand,
Or go, alone. O FATHER! take my hand,
             And through the throng
             Lead safe along
                    Thy child.

The cross is heavy, FATHER! I have borne
So long, and still do bear it. Let my worn
And fainting spirit rise to that bless'd land
Where crowns are given. FATHER, take my hand,
             And reaching down
             Lead to the crown
                    Thy child.

THE PILGRIM.

THE RESPONSE.

The way is dark, My child! but leads to light;
I would not have thee always walk by sight;
My dealings, now, thou canst not understand:
I meant it so ; but I will take thy hand,
   And through the gloom
   Lead safely home
     My child.

The day goes fast, My child! but is the night
Darker to Me than day ? In Me is light;
Keep close to Me, and every spectral band
Of fears shall vanish ! I will take thy hand,
   And through the night
   Lead up to light
     My child.

The way is long, my child! but it shall be
Not one step longer than is best for thee ;
And thou shalt know, at last, when thou shalt
 stand
Close to the gate, how I did take thy hand,
   And quick and straight
   Led to Heaven's gate
     My child.

THE PILGRIM.

The path is rough, My child! but, O, how sweet
Will be the rest for weary pilgrims meet!
When thou shalt reach the borders of that land
To which I lead thee, as I take thy hand,
   And safe, and blest,
    With Me shall rest
     My child.

The throng is great, My child! but at thy side
Thy FATHER walks! then be not terrified,
For I am with thee; will thy foes command
To let thee freely pass; will take thy hand,
   And through the throng
   Lead safe along
     My child.

The cross is heavy, child! yet there is One
Who bore a heavier for *thee*—My SON,
My well-beloved. With Him bear thine, and stand
With Him at last, and from thy FATHER's hand,
   Thy cross laid down,
   Receive thy crown,
     My child.

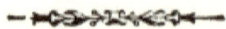

The Departed Nigh.

DEPARTED, say we? is it
    Departed, or Come nigh?
Dear friends in CHRIST more visit
    Than leave us when they die.
What thin veil still may hide them
    Some little sickness rends,
And, lo! we stand beside them:
    Are they *departed* friends?

Their dews on Zion mountain
    Our Hermon hills bedew;
Their river from the Fountain
    Flows down to meet us too.
The oil on the head, and under,
    Down to the skirts hath run;
And though we seem asunder,
    We still in CHRIST are one.

THE DEPARTED NIGH.

The many tides of ocean
    Are one vast tidal wave,
That sweeps, in landward motion,
    Alike to coast and cave;
And Life, from CHRIST outflowing,
    Is one wave evermore
To earth's dark caverns going,
    Or heaven's bright pearly shore.

Hail, perfected immortals!
    Even now we bid you hail;
We at the blood-stain'd portals,
    And *ye* within the veil!
The thin cloud-veil between us
    Is mere dissolving breath,
One heavens surround and screen us;
    And where art thou, O Death?

                      W. B. R.

This I Did for Thee—What Doest Thou for Me?

I GAVE My life for thee,
    My precious blood I shed,
That thou might'st ransomed be,
    And quickened from the dead.
I gave My life for thee;
What hast *thou* given for *Me?*

I spent long years for *thee,*
    In weariness and woe,
That an eternity
    Of joy *thou* mightest know.
I spent long years for *thee;*
Hast *thou* spent *one* for *Me?*

My FATHER's house of light,
    My rainbow-circled throne,
I left for earthly night,
    For wanderings sad and lone.
I left it all for *thee;*
Hast *thou* left aught for *Me?*

THIS I DID FOR THEE—WHAT DOEST THOU FOR ME?

I suffered much for *thee*,
    More than thy tongue may tell,
Of bitterest agony,
    To rescue *thee* from hell.
I suffered much for *thee;*
What doest *thou* bear for *Me?*

And I have brought to *thee*,
    Down from My home above,
Salvation full and free,
    My pardon and My love.
Great gifts I brought to *thee;*
What hast *thou* brought to *Me?*

O, let thy life be given,
    Thy years for Me be spent,
World-fetters all be riven,
    And joy with suffering blent:
Give thou *thyself* to Me,
And I will welcome thee.

He Knows.

I know not what may befall me,
God spreads a mist before mine eyes;
At every step in my onward path
He maketh new scenes to rise;
And every joy He sends me
Comes with a sudden and strange surprise.

I see not a step before me
As I tread on another year,
But the past is still in God's keeping,
The future His mercy will clear,
And what looks dark in the distance
May brighten as it grows near.

It may be the bitter future
Is less bitter than I think,
The Lord may sweeten the waters
Before I come to drink—
Or if Marah must be Marah
He will stand Himself by the brink.

'HE KNOWS.'

It may be He is keeping
For the coming of my feet,
Some gift of such rare blessedness,—
Some joy so strangely sweet,
That my lips will only tremble
The thanks they cannot speak.

Oh blessed, happy ignorance!
'Tis better not to know,
It keeps me so still in the tender arms
That will not let me go,—
It hushes my soul to rest
On the bosom that loves me so.

And so I go on not knowing
I would not if I might;
I'd rather walk in the dark with God
Than go alone in the light,
I'd rather walk with Him by faith
Than go alone by sight.

My heart shrinks back from the trials
The future may disclose,
Yet I never had a sorrow
But what the dear Lord chose;
So I force the coming tears back
With the whispered word, 'He knows.'

Going Home.

'GOING home,' and going quickly!
    It's a thought to cheer the heart,
    Should we suffer,—be it meekly;—
Soon the world and we must part,
Never more to meet again:
There's an end of suffering then,
There's an end of all that grieves us;
How the hope of this relieves us!

'Going home,'—how sweet, how cheering!
    Going to the place we love,
There in royal state appearing,
    'Midst the shining hosts above;
There our FATHER dwells and reigns,
Greater He than fancy feigns;
There His people live for ever,
Theirs a portion failing never!

'Going home,'—there's nothing dearer
    To the pilgrim's heart than '*home:*'
Drawing nearer still and nearer
    To the place where pilgrims come;
Much he thinks of what will be,
Much of what he hopes to see;
Thinks of kindred, friends, and brothers,
But of CHRIST above all others.

GOING HOME.

'Tis the blessed hope of seeing
   Him he loves, in glory there!
Blessed hope of ever being
   With the LORD, His joys to share :—
'Tis this hope that lightens toil,
And in sorrow makes him smile,
Cheers him in the midst of strangers,
Keeps him when beset with dangers.

'Going home,'—then it behoves us
   Here to live as pilgrims do :
When the trial comes, it proves us—
   Proves if we have faith or no.
Let us make our calling sure,
Let us to the end endure ;
In the SAVIOUR's love abiding,
In the SAVIOUR's *strength* confiding!

C. F

Taylor's Large-Type Christian Library.

Any of these Volumes sent post-free for the published price in stamps

Marshall's Gospel Mystery of Sanctification. (New Edition.) With Memoir of the Author. Cloth 3s. 6d.

'I know not if I ever spoke to you of *Marshall on Sanctification*. He is at present my daily companion; nor do I know an Author who sets forth the Gospel in a way so suited to promote the conjoint interests of peace and holiness.'— Dr CHALMERS.

Baxter's Saints' Everlasting Rest. Cloth, 3s. 6d.

'The Best Edition of "The Saints' Rest" with which we are acquainted.'—*Editor of Christian Treasury.*

Owen on the Glory of Christ, in His Person, Office, and Work. Cloth, 3s. 6d.

'An admirable book—equal to anything Howe or Baxter has written—Owen's Masterpiece.'—Dr JOHN BROWN.

'Grace and Truth' under Twelve Aspects. By Dr W. P. MACKAY, Hull. (New extra large-type edition.) Cloth, 3s. 6d.

Booth's Reign of Grace, from its Rise to its Consummation. With Introductory Essay, by Dr CHALMERS. Cloth, 2s. 6d.

Olney Hymns. By COWPER and NEWTON. (New Edition.) Cloth, 2s. 6d.

Romaine's Select Letters. (Fifth Edition.) Cloth, 2s. 6d.

One Hundred Choice Hymns. Cloth.

Rawlin on Christ the Righteousness of His People. Edited by Professor LUMSDEN. Cloth, 2s.

'A spring of living water drawn from the Fountain one hundred and twelve years ago. Has merits which will stand the test of generations yet to come.'—*Witness.*

Autobiography of Robert Flockhart, the Street Preacher. Edited by THOMAS GUTHRIE, D.D. With Reminiscences by Rev. JAMES ROBERTSON. Cloth, 2s.; Cheap Edition, 1s.

Willison on the Sanctification of the Sabbath. Cloth, 2s.; Cheap Edition, 1s.

Dyer's Christ's Famous Titles, and a Believer's Golden Chain. Cloth, 2s.

The Christian Cabinet for 1879, containing Narratives, Hymns, and Gospel Gems. Cloth, 1s. 6d.

———— Volumes of former years may still be had.

Taylor's Large-Type Christian Library.

'Grace and Truth' under Twelve Aspects. By Dr W. P. MACKAY, Hull. Cloth, 2s.; also in bevelled boards, gilt edges, 3s.; Cheap Edition, 1s.
LETTER from the Rev. CANON RYLE, M.A. :—
18th Aug. 1875.
'DEAR DR MACKAY,—I cannot help telling you how very much I like your "Grace and Truth;" the first chapter especially is worth its weight in Gold. I do not hesitate to say that I have seen no book so likely to do good as your "Grace and Truth" for many a long day. May God bless it!—Yours sincerely in Christ,—J. C. RYLE.'

Charnock's Weak Grace Victorious. Cloth, 1s. 6d.

Guthrie's Christian's Great Interest; or, The Trial of a Saving Interest in Christ, Cloth, 1s. 6d.
'The best book I ever read on the subject.'—Dr CHALMERS.

Closing Scenes in Humble Life. By J. C. S. With Introductory Note by Rev. JOHN MACPHERSON, Author of 'Life of Duncan Mathieson,' etc. Cloth, 1s.

Memoirs and Manuscript of Isobel Hood. By the late Rev. JOHN MACDONALD, Calcutta. With Introductory Notice by HUGH MILLER. (New Edition.) Cloth, 1s.

A Token of Remembrance for the Young. By the late Rev. DAVID SMITH, D.D., Biggar. With Memoir by JOHN KER, D.D., Glasgow. (New Edition.) Cloth, 1s.

The Way to Zion. By DR ANDREW BONAR and others. Cloth, 1s.

Diary of Ann Smith, a Plain Country-woman. With Memoir by the late Rev. WM. SMART, Linlithgow, and Preface by Rev. Dr SMITH, Biggar. (Fifth Edition.) Cloth, 1s.

Seven Gems. By Rev. R. M. M'CHEYNE. Cloth, 1s.

Mason's Songs of Praise and Penitential Cries. Cloth, 1s.

On Time, and the End of Time. By JOHN FOXE, the Martyrologist. Cloth, 1s.

Rays of Consolation from a Swiss Valley. By Pasteur CH. CHATELANAT, Pasteur of Aigle, Canton de Vaud. Translated by LADY HOBART. Cloth, 8d.

Heavenly Light Streaming from the Cross. By MISS HERDMAN, of Melrose. Cloth, 6d.

Dyer's Golden Chain of Twenty Links for a Believer to wear round his neck. Limp Cloth, 4d.

www.ingramcontent.com/pod-product-compliance
Lightning Source LLC
Chambersburg PA
CBHW031825230426
43669CB00009B/1228